MORE DIMENSIONS THAN YOU KNOW

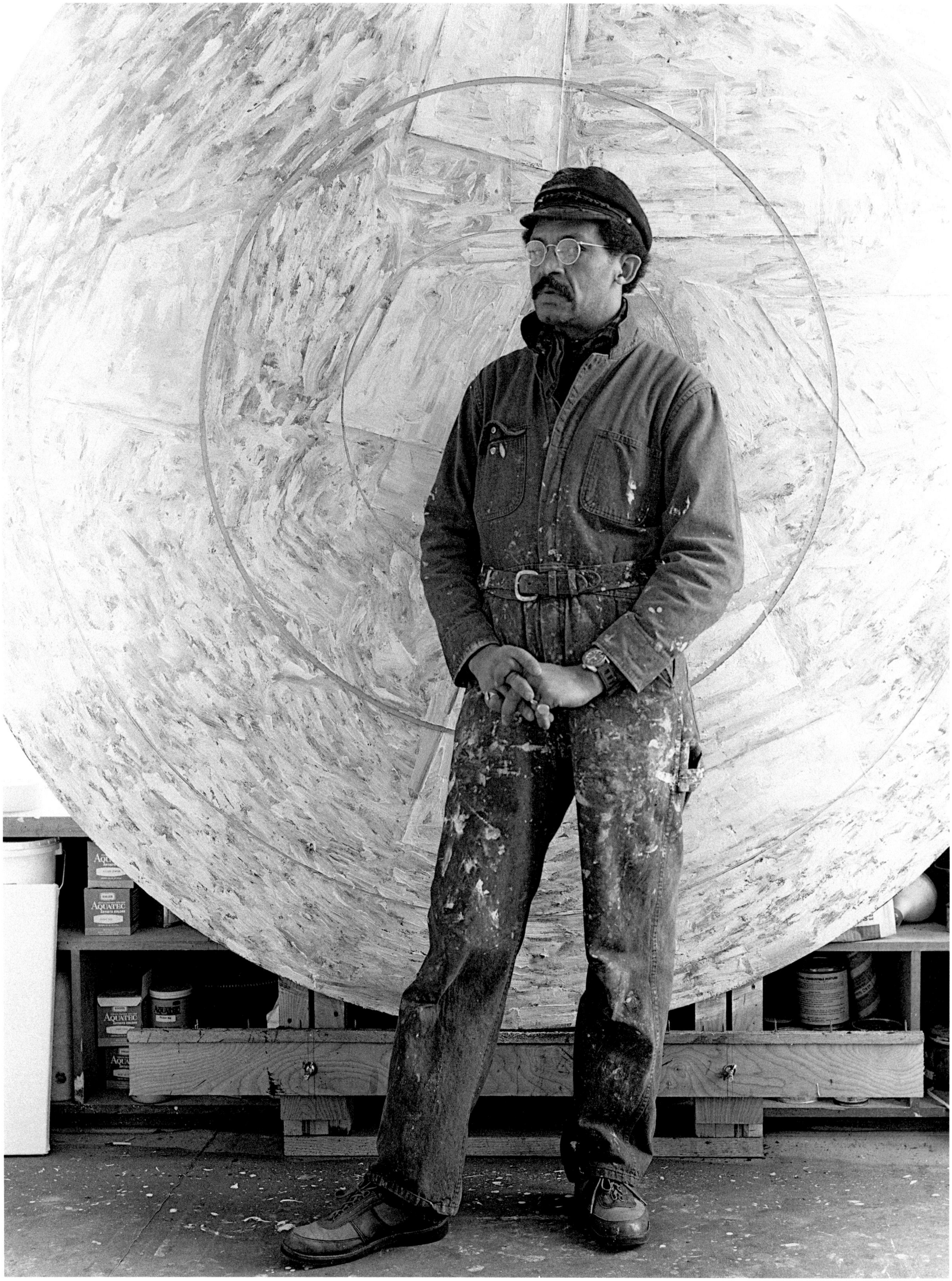
AQUATEC
AQUATEC
AQUATEC

MORE DIMENSIONS THAN YOU KNOW
JACK WHITTEN, PAINTINGS 1979–1989

Richard Shiff

Hauser & Wirth Publishers

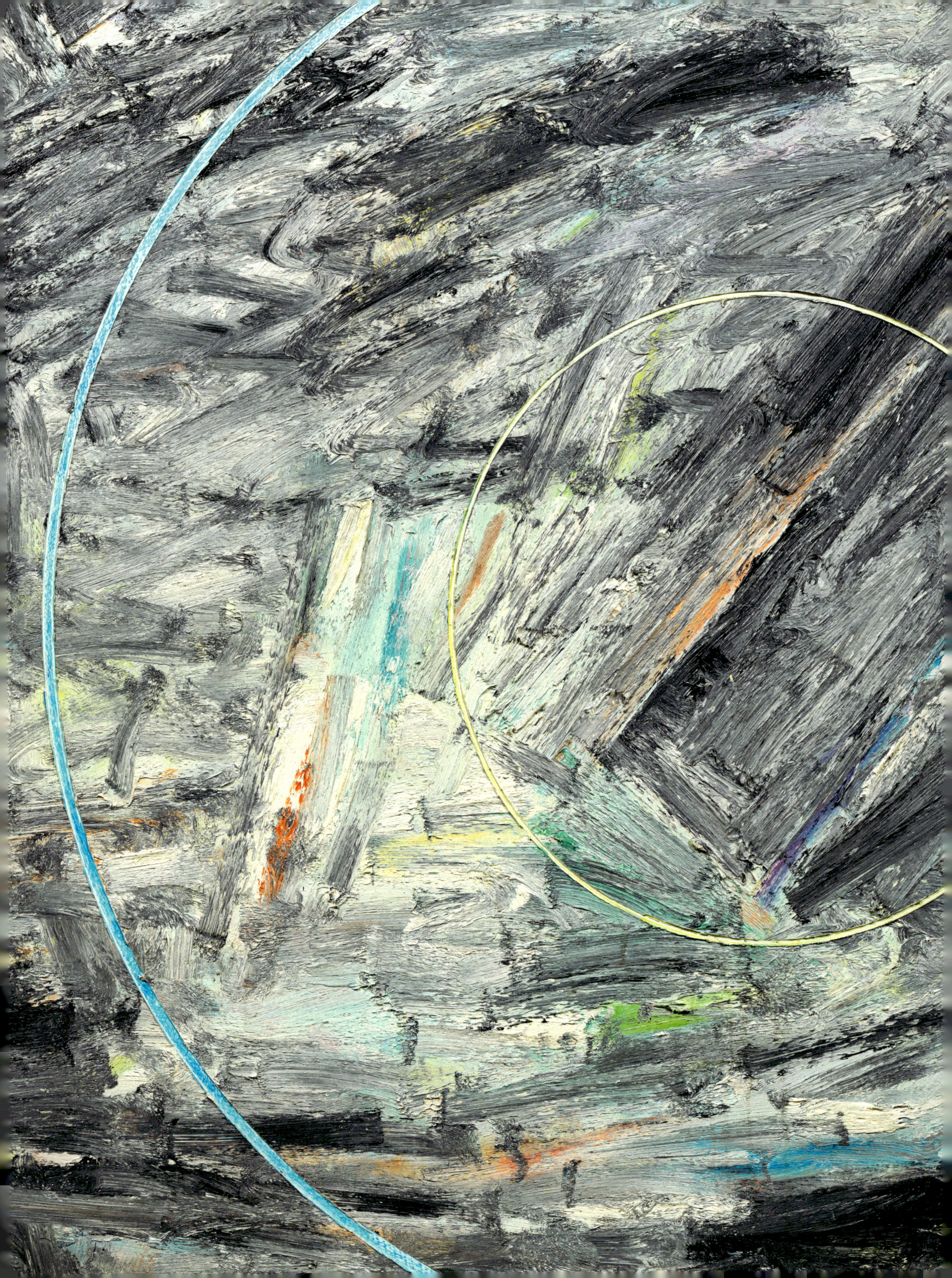

Art must satisfy a very specific personal longing for universality. A desire to feel completely satisfied. A part of the total structure of things. Abstraction is the only possibility for this type of satisfaction, with figuration we are forever depicting something other than the rock-bottom meaning of universality. For this technological age abstraction is the language.

– October 24, 1979

I depend both upon the spiritual and the material out of psychic necessity.

– January 22, 1986

I consider myself to be part of nature. I am not in competition with nature. I am simply a part, an important part, but not more important than Mt. Everest or the common sparrow. Nature is everything conceivable to the human mind.

– April 12, 1986

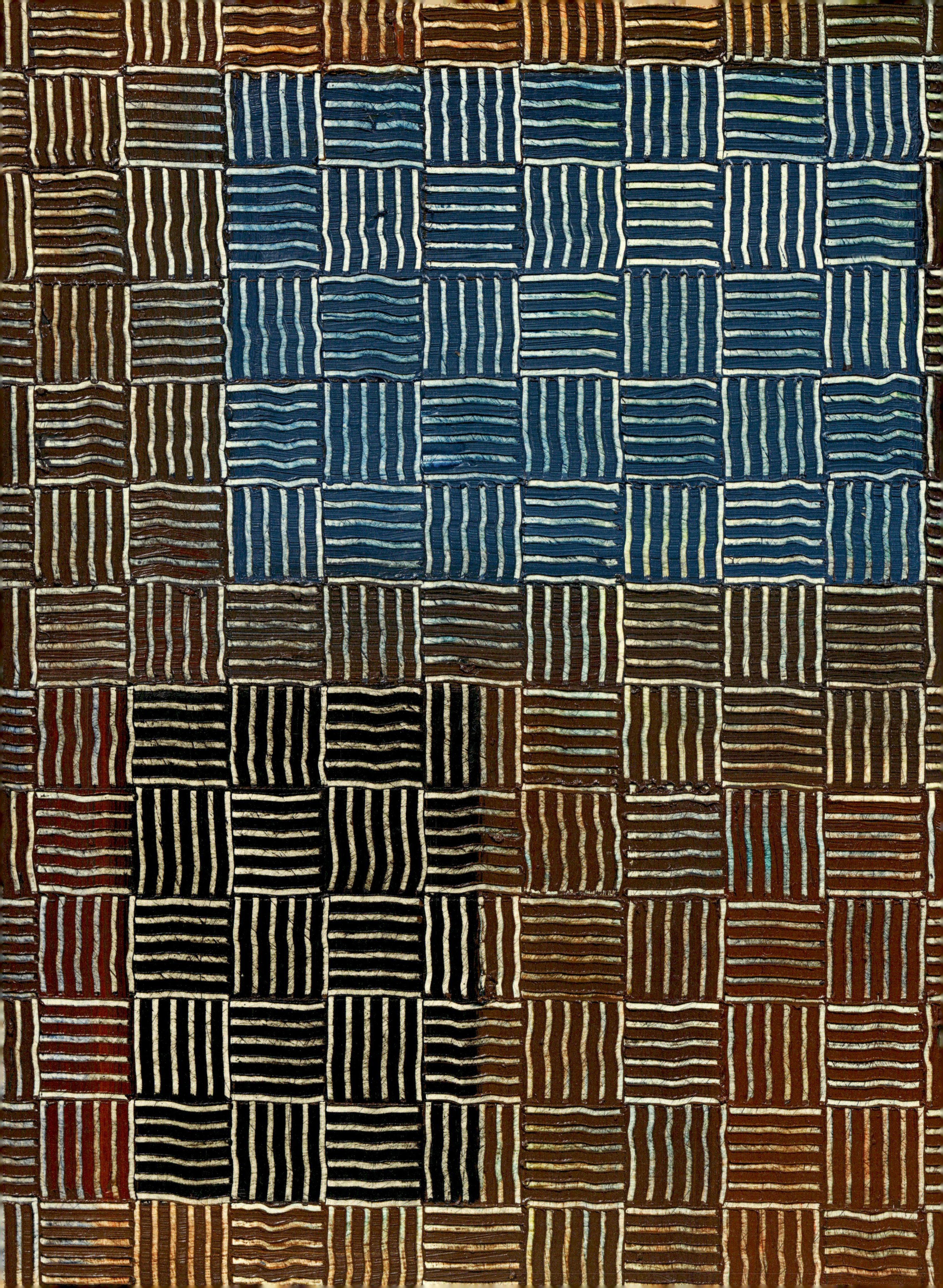

IMAGE THAT COMES OUT OF MATTER

Richard Shiff

"Jack Whitten has an agenda. My agenda right from the beginning is to change the course of painting through innovation."[1] Concepts and classifications must defer to innovation. The product of more than half a century's work, Jack Whitten's accomplishment in painting still lacks a category. I imagine his aesthetic development as a course apart from the evolution of art registered in the critical discourse of the late twentieth and early twenty-first centuries. Neither analysis by formal composition nor interpretation by historical context suits what he does. An alternative critique, analysis by process, fares better.

Whitten's painting derives from the classical modernism of Paul Cézanne, Pablo Picasso, and Jackson Pollock: "My position has always been one of working through the mainstream of Western art. My objective is one of projection, that is, to deflect, to bend, to hammer out a form dependent upon the dictates of my sensibility."[2] The "projection" is not of an image available to be exposed, as in projecting a film or expressing a formulated thought. Rather, Whitten projects a process. The process becomes the "form" that must be "hammer[ed] out." It becomes the image. Whitten brings his thought full circle: "I am the process," he affirmed in 1983.[3] Artist, process, form, image: if only the links were conceptually secure.

Because Whitten identifies with a process instead of a product, his reference to "sensibility," a notion he often invokes, may confuse analysis. Customarily, we reduce sensibility to identity, as if biographical factors of race, gender, ethnicity, class, education, and age would reveal everything of relevance not otherwise apparent. We are the products of the data of our lives. But the process that both guides and is exposed by Whitten's art is human perception, which has no personal biography: "Perception is the common

Untitled II, 1979, detail

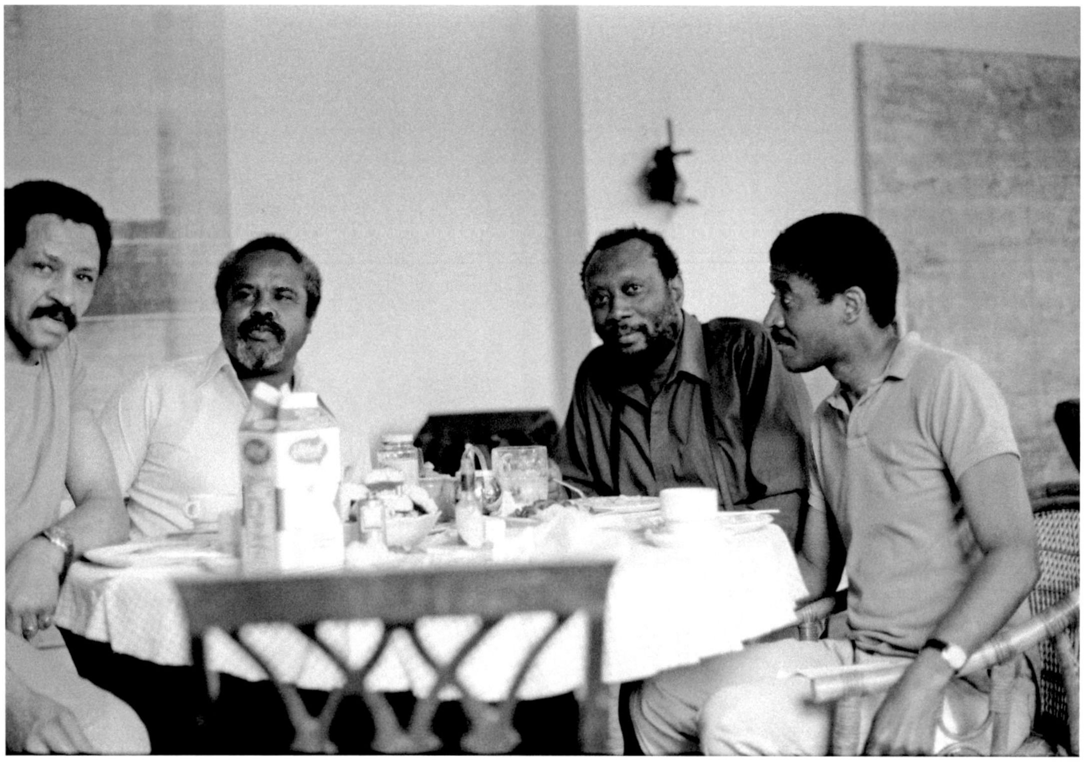

Jack Whitten, Mel Edwards, Frank Bowling, and Bill Williams in the Whitten family living room, 36 Lispenard St., New York, 1983

denominator [shared by] artists from different cultural backgrounds, geographical locations, ethnicities, spiritualities, and sexual orientations."[4] No documentation suggests that a forty-year-old African American, raised in Alabama and residing in New York, ought to have been painting *Untitled II* in 1979 (pp. 6, 43). Whitten has a sophisticated sense of his black identity and is well aware of his position in the political and social order; yet *Untitled II*, like most of his oeuvre, offers no coherent personal or political narrative to be read from the pattern, texture, and color of its surface. If a narrative were to be discerned, the work would be classified accordingly. Art slotted into categories is unlikely to "change the course of painting" or change anything.

We can project, just as Whitten can. We can stereotype him as a black artist of the Civil Rights era, or a latter-day New York abstractionist, or a conceptually oriented process artist, or even, in view of *Untitled II*, a pattern painter of the 1970s. We can project him into any one of these unproblematic positions, inserting him into a social history and an art history already constituted. But the results will seem strained and unsatisfying for anyone who has had a phenomenological experience of Whitten's art. He referred to his "projection" as a continuing "objective"—a process. This was in 1989. The process must have been, and must still be, innovative; the forms attained have not yet rejoined the "mainstream of Western art."

INNOVATION

In a trivial sense, everyone is an innovator. Most often, our moments of innovation merely signal a difference from prevailing norms. We offer novel solutions to problems that only prove unworkable, and conditions remain as they were. Some innovations, however, change the orientation of a discipline or practice in ways that affect others, who cannot conceptualize what has happened. An effect, rather than its explanation, constitutes the meaning of what Whitten accomplishes. A log of the artist's intellectual responses to his aesthetic experience includes the following introspective passage from 1979; here, social concerns merge with inspiration from the physical sciences, all leading to hope for enhanced human consciousness, a more acute process of perception:

> The organic substance of seeing . . . happens when opposites cancel out. The electromagnetic field comes close to giving a physical example of what happens in the process of vision. I think that my growing up black in America gives me an advantage in dealing with the unique psychology of vision. I am a product of the cancellation of opposing races. . . . I don't feel it to be my job as an artist to unravel the psychological mysteries of being. As an artist, I merely present and dare not explain! . . . Those people who are capable of seeing will see, and the others must be content with the trash of our technological society. As we progress *into technology*, so will our desire *to see* increase.[5]

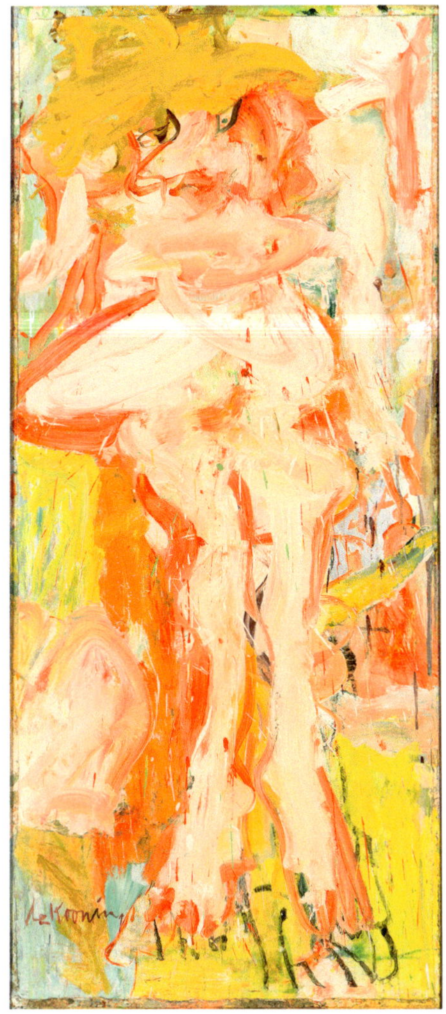

Willem de Kooning, *Woman Accabonac*, 1966. Oil on paper mounted on canvas, 79 x 35⅛ in. (200.7 x 89.2 cm). Whitney Museum of American Art, New York; purchase, with funds from the artist and Mrs. Bernard F. Gimbel, 67.75

The correspondence between these thoughts about human perception and Whitten's personal etiology is multi-dimensional. With regard to the "cancellation of opposing races," he may have been considering his life as a black man within white Euro-American culture: Alabama tempered by New York, New York tempered by Alabama. This individual history generated a "special sensibility."[6] Whitten spent the formative years of his youth living under "American Apartheid" in the South, followed by an education at Manhattan's Cooper Union—he enrolled in fall 1960—and a career in, or at the edge of, the school of modernist painting.[7] As a young artist in New York, he was mentored by both white and black members of the abstract expressionist generation, including Willem de Kooning and Norman Lewis (above and p. 10): "Can you imagine what this meant for me? I'm getting information from both sides of the [racial] divide and, believe me, we're talking a

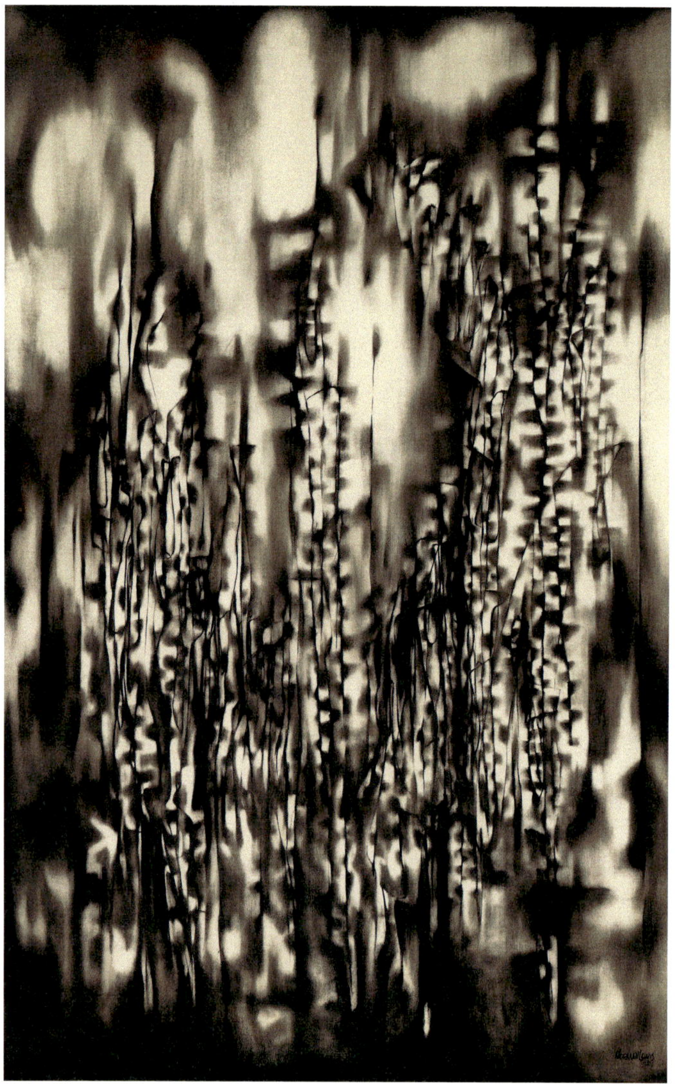

Norman Lewis, *Every Atom Glows: Electrons in Luminous Vibration*, 1951. Oil on canvas, 54 x 35 in. (137.2 x 88.9 cm). Museum of Fine Arts, Boston; The John Axelrod Collection—Frank B. Bemis Fund, Charles H. Bayley Fund, and The Heritage Fund for a Diverse Collection, 2011.1799

divide."[8] Whitten endured a split culture; most of his invitations to exhibit entailed showing with other black artists. But he also believed that his art crossed social and psychological boundaries. The effect of division on the perception of a situation can be overcome with adjustments to perception itself. "Identity, race, politics, sexuality are all crutches," he has said: "They are illusionary signposts designed by culture that obscure deeper elemental truths. . . . Think of the most powerful electron microscope capable of seeing the structure of feeling. This is the genesis of perception."[9]

The study of perception, not its mere reflection in illustrative imagery, became Whitten's self-assignment as a visual artist. In 1964, he had an epiphany, virtually an out-of-body moment that he felt compelled to verbalize in the following way: "The image is photographic. Therefore, I must photograph my thoughts."[10] What the statement may indicate is hardly clear; I offer some speculation at the conclusion of this essay. For now, consider Whitten's vision of a photographic practice—photographing his mind, his perception—as having determined the course of his material experimentation from that moment onward.

While some of his contemporaries identified themselves as photorealists and replicated the *look* of photography, Whitten made objects that embodied a *process* analogous to photographic technology. Other painters produced "pictures," images that referred beyond their immediate presence to something external in place and time—something absent—even if only another photographic image (as in Andy Warhol's use of the news media and celebrity press as his subject matter). To the contrary, Whitten created a material object conceived not to refer in the sense of depicting, but to become its own image, even when it served as a personal memorial, as in *The Gift: Dedicated to the Memory of Packy* (1988 [opposite and pp. 80–83]).[11] The human tragedy of Packy, a student of Whitten's who died prematurely, may well be signaled by what the artist describes as a "breakdown" in the surface of the

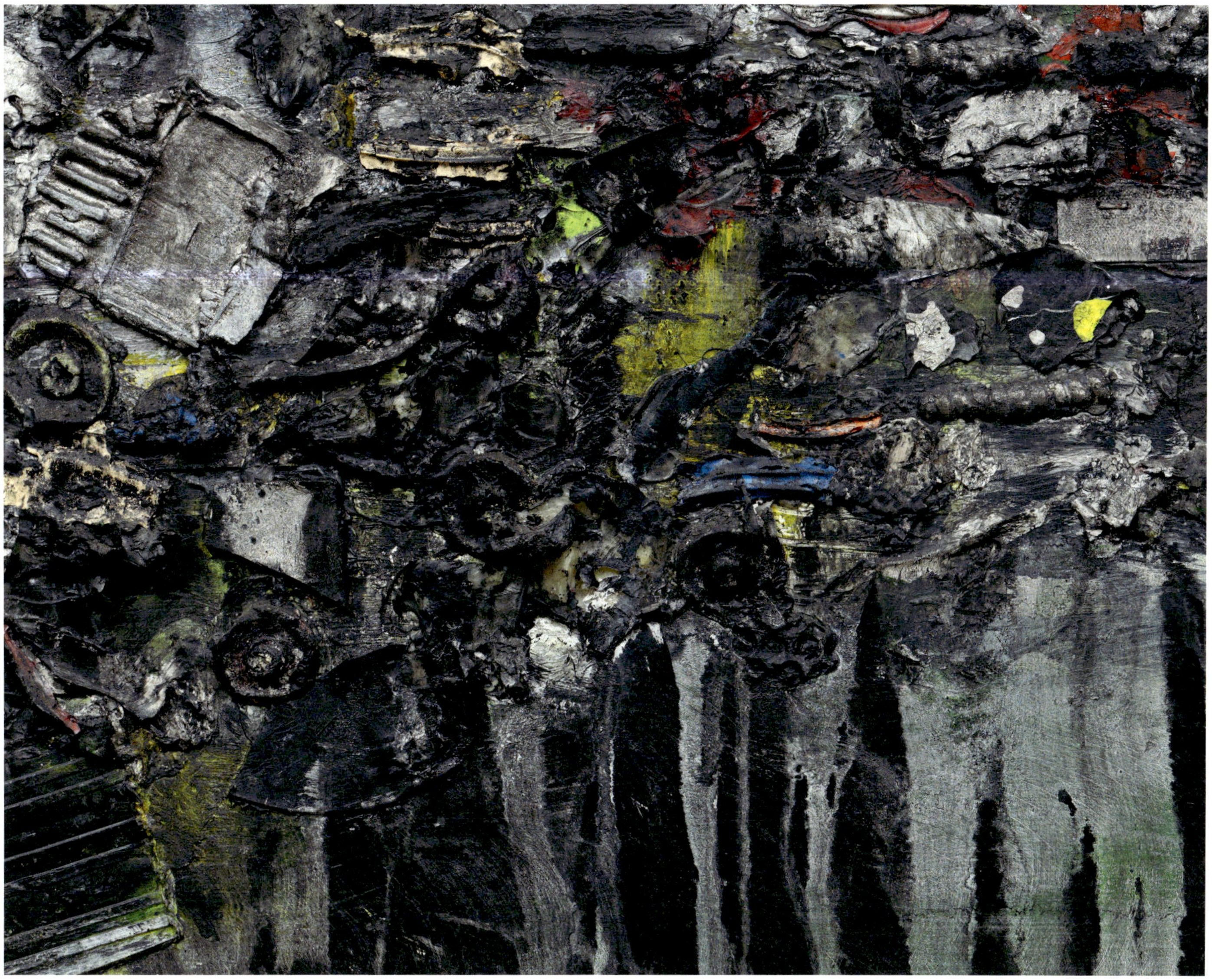

The Gift: Dedicated to the Memory of Packy, 1988, detail

work.[12] An area of fragments of acrylic appears to be disintegrating, even melting, within the local context of the painting. Yet the metaphor should not be pursued beyond a vague suggestion: no image of the person Packy emerges. Perhaps Whitten had works like *The Gift* in mind when he cautioned himself regarding metaphoric content: "The image comes from the material. . . . I must remove the metaphor, whatever it may be."[13]

Whitten posed a question for himself: "How do you [memorialize a person or event] without resorting to purely illustrational devices? . . . The way I try to attempt this, is to use the material to transfer this information."[14] The means of transferring information is by a code of translation and a device of transmission, from one language and location to another language and location. The fragments of acrylic in *The Gift* are too irregular to articulate a language; they have no

E Stamp VI Vouvray (For Harvey Quaytman), 2008. Acrylic on canvas, 42¼ x 42¼ in. (107.3 x 107.3 cm). Kravis Collection

readily apparent code. But the physical performance of these elements displaces their illustrative function.[15] Typically, Whitten's "information" is not a biographical or historical fact but a set of feelings, a complex of sensations and emotions. He is the painter, yet the paint does much of the acting. Actions induce feelings, just as feelings induce actions. Although feelings for the person known as Packy guided some of Whitten's constructive choices when he created *The Gift*, all of his work of the 1980s had a broader purpose. He has stated his intent, referring to both past and future: "I'm desperately looking for something to make painting signify contemporary thought. I've often thought of science as an analogy. So the code system, even though they're mechanical codes, fits my purposes to make painting contemporary."[16] Photography is a product of science, and its operation depends on the coding of light.

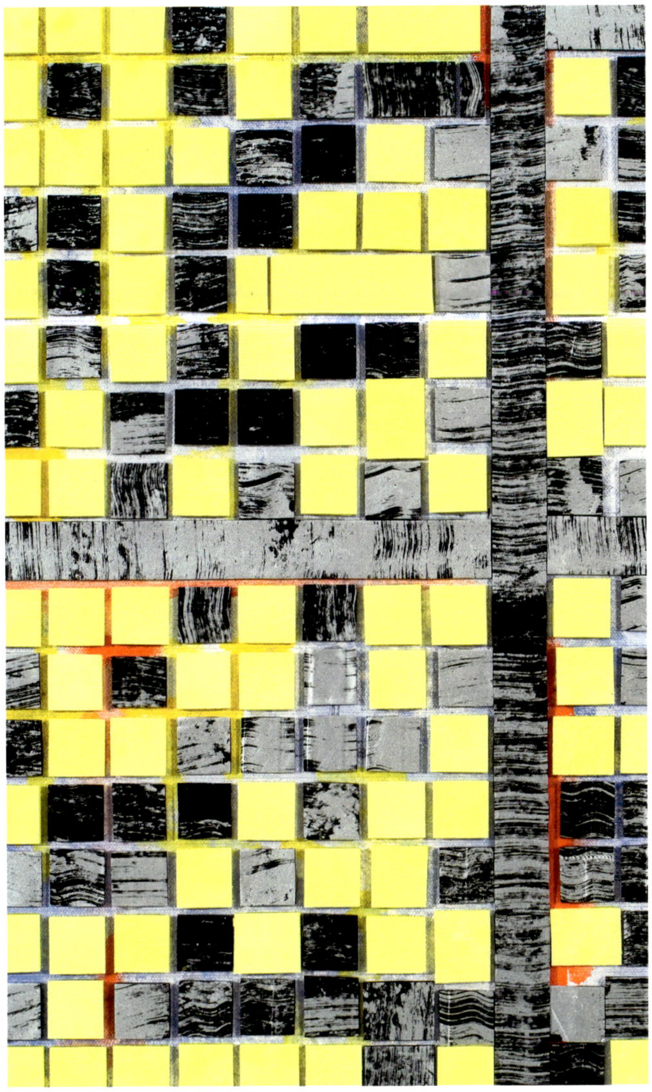

E Stamp VI Vouvray (For Harvey Quaytman), detail

Whitten's remark about signifying the contemporary mentality occurs in a lengthy interview of 2009. His immediate reference was his series of E-stamp images, each dedicated to an individual (as was *The Gift*). He had recently completed *E Stamp VI Vouvray (For Harvey Quaytman)* (2008 [opposite and above]). Its pixel-like elements derive from grids designed for electronic scanning; in terms of a photographic model, the analogy would be to digital photography, not analog. Whitten had his private reasons for linking each of the E-stamp series to its designee; in the case of Quaytman, yellowish Vouvray wine was an association.[17] E-stamps are normally black-and-white; to produce their likes in an arbitrary set of colors, one has only to preserve the contrast of dark and light. As for viewers, they need not factor in metaphorical content (the wine) or a chromatic transformation. The image is not of an E-stamp, but of a range of feeling, and follows a code as emotional as it is material. Although the distribution of elements may adhere to a pattern of digital coding, the heft of the physical presence of Whitten's acrylic hardly relates to the flat print of an actual E-stamp. As if caught mid-point in the process, Whitten's form is matter that generates its image, whereas an E-stamp is image alone. Each of the gridded acrylic elements of *E Stamp VI*—Whitten calls them "tesserae"—consists of a volume of matter. Because the individual block of paint has been cut from a multi-layered slab, it conveys material information within it, not just on a surface that might be scanned, unit by unit. To put it differently, Whitten was converting dematerialized electronic information, the E-stamp grid, to a material source of a type from which most of our information is derived to begin with: physical matter. *E Stamp VI* assumes the disembodied form of coded information as an *effect*, which reverts to its *cause* in organic physicality. This amounts to an inversion of the technology—and as painting, an innovation.

Whitten's recent statement of intent—"to make painting signify contemporary thought"—is consistent with the previously quoted studio note from 1979, in which the painter compares the play of vision to an "electromagnetic field" and invokes "science as an analogy." His aesthetic innovation appears to turn inward to his "sensibility" as it probes "contemporary thought." Yet technology—mechanical and electronic, materialized and dematerialized—has done much to form his sensibility. "As we progress *into technology*," he says with emphasis, we will want, and be able, to see more ("so will our desire *to see* increase").[18] Here, innovation in art appears as a check on progress in technology. Whitten implies that developments in technological imaging external to the fine arts, on which contemporary thought depends, require an artist to assess the new imaging for its effect on human perception. An artist investigates actively what a culture has already accepted passively: "The modern technological society depends upon the fast movement of vast amounts of complex diversified data; this exerts extreme psychological pressures upon each of us. Artists continually invent ways to deal with these pressures as a means of survival."[19]

Whitten's technology of painting amounts to a process executed by hand—though in odd ways—and performed through the body. Both viscerally and psychically, it affects a viewer's sensibility (mine, at least), if only because the nature of the artist's engagement of hand, body, and matter is so unexpected. His art incorporates the speed, technical efficiency, and capacity to carry "diversified data" that he and others associate with the contemporary environment. An art of these qualities becomes one of social "survival." Yet one might think that during the 1980s the culture of the fine arts, caught up in critical negativity, had little will to survive. Whitten must have seemed to be working in the wrong medium. Artists committed to painting received diminished attention from critics, with the exception of those who exaggerated their brushwork through figural distortion—a technique directed at increasing the sense of personal expression in a return to older modes of modernist art. To recuperate the past as a way of demonstrating that nothing changes fundamentally, save by ideological revolution that no individual can influence, is self-defeating. This negative syndrome inhibits invention, encouraging insignificant variation rather than innovation. Some painters of the 1980s were reproducing the entire history of the medium as parody—often referred to as "appropriation art"—and reducing various methods to pastiche. Whether bombastically expressive (Julian Schnabel) or crudely parodic (Mike Bidlo), the "new" figuration of the 1980s was endlessly referential and ironical. Though irony may be the prevalent trope within the past century of art—beginning with Picasso and Marcel Duchamp in their antithetical ways—Whitten's art has seldom, if ever, been marked by it. By this standard alone, he is already unusual. When he referred to his continuing innovation, it was no idle boast, nor an idealist's fantasy.

Yet, especially during the 1980s, critics of art argued that innovation itself was fantasy. Many artists were investigating photography in novel ways (Cindy Sherman, Richard Prince), but with the aim of subverting the clichés of its imagery, not the operation of its mechanism. Originality, innovation, sincere expression—these concepts became so suspect as to be taboo in many circles, and may still be.[20] Any pretense to original imagery was likely to provoke mockery on the part of commentators caught up in the intellectual fashion of those years. To counter assertions of innovation, American critics claimed support in the traditions of both analytical and continental philosophy; they sometimes invoked Ludwig Wittgenstein's sense of language as tautological, and more often Jacques Derrida's deconstruction of language as an individual expression of uniquely contextual meaning.[21] By analogy to the dematerialized verbal signs of language, the material signs of the visual arts were described as caught in a web of endless repetition—like a photographic cliché, the negative of innumerable positives. Artists were reduced to copying each other. In 1980, an influential critic wrote of the "fantasy that art is free of other discourses, institutions, free, above all, of history," a fantasy maintained when "every work of art is held to be absolutely unique and original."[22]

Innovation and originality are not equivalent concepts. The first pertains to procedures, the second to results. And Whitten never regarded his innovations as "free, above all, of history." There was an exception: "I am free of *art* history," he wrote in 1979.[23] He criticized the tradition of art for having separated "the idea, the concept, the execution [within] painting as an activity"; conventional painting and its commentary located cultural meaning in the image (with originality a factor), as opposed to the medium that generated the image (involved with procedure).[24] In contradistinction, Whitten's concern has been the technology of imaging and its performance, not the picture it produces. He characterizes conventional painting this way: "There's an idea and then one proceeds to illustrate it. I want something where the idea is not separated from the action."[25] He wants the process. His elaboration of this thought merits lengthy quotation:

> We are familiar with things being either/or, abstract or representational, but there's a third order out there that's not abstract, nor is it representation.... You have to go beyond the notion of just bringing them together. It's ... an image that comes out of matter.... I'm aware of something being caught in the matter. But again, the difficult part is, how do you direct it, how do you construct it? If it's not an illustration of something, then what is it? This thing has its own mind, its own body. It's similar to [African] animists who believe that all matter holds something in it.... There's a relation here when I speak of spirit and matter. That it is possible to direct something in the matter.[26]

At the time of this searching statement, Whitten was about to begin a work dedicated to the memory of the African American congresswoman Barbara Jordan. He told his interviewer, Jeanne Siegel: "She's in that bucket [of acrylic]! I have put her in there through the spirit."[27] In an animistic way, Jordan's spirit or soul would emerge as an image from the surface-matter of Whitten's canvas; yet the work would be neither metaphorical nor referential by any other means, at least not in the artist's conception of it. An image coming out of matter would facilitate the communication of Jordan's soul with Whitten's, just as Packy's soul and Whitten's had communicated. We should not try to reason our way to this reality. "The power is within me," the painter wrote in 1987: "It must come directly from the soul unhindered by logic."[28]

POLITICS OF ART

"I have successfully made a breakthrough from the gravitational field of Art History," Whitten stated in 1979.[29] To have somehow moved beyond the pull of art history did not mean that he had escaped other forces. His aesthetic interests are embedded in the social history of his race and its diaspora: "When the question of being a Black artist comes up, I always say we have to go to the word 'sensibility.' ... Slavery eliminated our sense of place. Blacks had no choice but to recreate a sense of place."[30] To this, he associates paintings denoted by the term *Site*, as well as others that develop a casting or imprinting technique analogous to three-dimensional copying. To create works such as *Soweto Disk II AKA Big O for Obama* (1985 [pp. 57–59]), *Site IV* (1986 [pp. 69–71]), and *The Offering* (1989 [pp. 88, 90]), Whitten cast material surfaces from the common environment—manhole covers, grillwork, the diamond plate of hatchway entrances, the tread of a tire or a shoe, items of food, bubble wrap. The combinations of their patterns, captured in three dimensions with embossed and debossed surfaces, convey a unique sense of place. Works of this type represent urban experience as "topographical" (Whitten's term)—surfaces that evoke spaces of multiple dimensions are configured as planes in low relief that must be viewed from numerous angles and distances. Low relief catches environmental light in the way that an actual site does, as opposed to a "frontal," pictorial image that uses devices of illusion to represent light.[31] To a great extent, conventional paintings deactivate light, merely reflecting it back from a uniform plane as opposed to articulating its substance. A "frontal" image mimics a world, as in a mirror; an acrylic collage in low relief constitutes a world in itself.

Whitten's presentations of places are antithetical to conventional representations of landscape, urban or otherwise. The artist refers to the surface of his Sites as "specific ground," a configuration—a collage—of elements constituting a unique material environment.[32]

Because each of the elements is cast from an existing surface, they are not representational in the usual sense, nor are they abstractions. Their form is indexical—Whitten might say "eidetic"—derived from the referent or source by direct contact, a type of causality.[33] No figurative distance separates a cast from its mold or a mold from its model. The connections are from positive to negative to positive, where the polarities could just as well be reversed (imagine deciding that an item of clothing looks better worn inside out—the negative becomes the positive).

Whitten's black sensibility remains in place just as American racism remains, fading from history only gradually, if at all. The break in tradition caused by the African diaspora continues to generate unrelieved anxiety.[34] Many other aspects of the cultural environment, whether related to blacks or to whites, change at appreciably faster rates. Whitten's aesthetic reacts to the rapid evolution of technological imaging, to which his art is an informed response: "My metaphors are found in scientific processes. Hydrogen bubble chambers turned me on in the '70s. Electronic scanning devices—that's where I found my images."[35] Yet as someone classified as a painter of hand-crafted "abstract art," Whitten was largely written out of the critical discourse of the 1980s, which favored practices engaged either with conceptual play or overtly politicized imagery. His acrylic configurations of "site" passed silently by critics who were expecting a more illustrative view of the black experience in America, which they had received from members of an older generation whom Whitten deeply admired, including the likes of Jacob Lawrence and Romare Bearden. "I got ten years of [solid] work out of the '80s," Whitten concluded; "but I realized that the works I was doing could not participate in the sort of thing that was going on."[36]

Those who denied progress in the arts implied somewhat paradoxically that work in the medium of painting, to the extent that it sought to develop new imagery, must be retrograde. By a logic of negation common at the time, innovation in painting would not be valued as a release from cultural convention, but rather as an arrogation of social authority on the part of the individual artist, an exclusive claim to the privilege of aesthetic freedom.[37] Yet what may seem politically retrograde from one perspective is just as readily perceived as a provocation to change—in Whitten's case, to reimagine phenomena that had been neglected or never noticed at all. A medium of visualization does not exhaust its potential so long as someone actively extends it. Personally, I like to think of retrogression as innovation in reverse—not so much a movement backward, but an inverting of priorities and expectations. Movement in any direction represents change, and change has consequences. Much of the innovative force of Whitten's art has involved inversion in many guises.

INVERSION

No longer immersed in the negativity of the 1980s, a critic today is more likely to accept Whitten's innovations at face value—at their *perceptual* value—rather than dismiss the artist's ambitions solely on theoretical grounds. We should look before we think. A realization has been guiding Whitten's effort: "Art more than anything in society has the power to change perception. . . . Change perception and we change reality."[38] The way we sense or look affects the way we think. From 1979 to 1989, Whitten produced a series of works aimed at stimulating perception to innovate its own being, to change of its own necessity. By means of the hand-oriented graphic medium of paint, he worked his way through media derived from photographic and photo-electronic technologies that would otherwise sideline the hand. Electronic (digital) photography was not commonplace during the 1980s; but Whitten had radar, cathode-ray scanning, electron microscopy, video, and many similar technologies to consider.[39]

Despite his remarkable range of manual skill, Whitten avoided work with a brush from 1970 forward. A major motivation was to escape the shadow of

Nee II, 1977. Acrylic on canvas, 64 x 64 in. (162.6 x 162.6 cm)

de Kooning's gestural mastery: "I made a vow that I'm [going to] stop doing those gestural paintings altogether. . . . My solution was to expand the gesture while taking my hand out of it."[40] During the 1970s, Whitten developed several effective methods. For works like *Nee II* (1977 [above]), he set a large canvas against a hard surface, having placed some slight objects underneath (perhaps cord or wire), then applied several layers of a bright titanium-white ground, and over this, an acrylic slip: "graphite, pure crystalline silica, and acrylic medium."[41] He raked the surface from a standing position in a single broad gesture (hands at a distance), using an improvised tool he called a "developer" or "processor" (for a small painting, he could use a hair comb). The raking removed approximately half of the slip or surface overlay, line by line, leaving an image to appear as if instantaneously, with the traces of the objects underneath being exposed in the corrugations.[42] Works of this type look like video screens with horizontal interference; but they are dimensional, not flat.

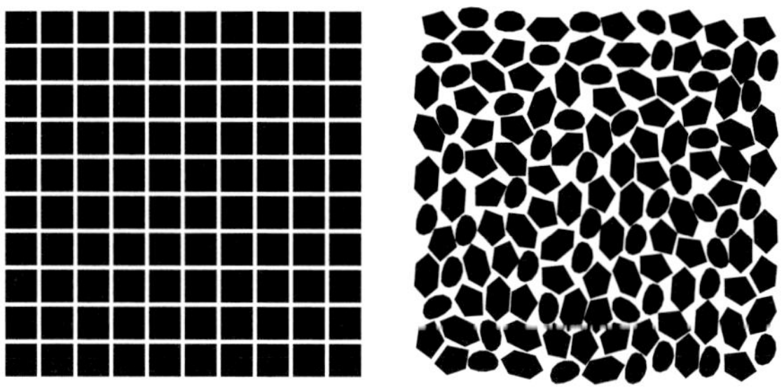

Schematic renderings show distribution of (left) pixels in digital photography and (right) emulsion in analog photography

The parallel lines of *Nee II* connote the raster of an electronic imaging system. In contrast, the scattering of variant grays between or beneath the lines resembles the irregular distribution of tone in the emulsion of analog photography. One system or code accords with the geometric rigidity of a digital grid; the other capitalizes on the organic flexibility of a chemical coating of irregular particles (above). Whitten's process alludes to the two types of photography, the photo-electronic and the photo-chemical. It also reflects the lesson that he drew from de Kooning: "Speed of gesture was the only way possible for him to capture the intensity of emotion. As a young painter interested in photography's influence on painting, I equated speed to the split second timing of the camera's shutter." To this, he adds: "Light was not only carried by paint but also trapped in a split second. . . . Bill [de Kooning's] brush stroke was fast but I had to go faster!"[43]

During the 1970s, the instant of technological time was being appropriated not only by the action of cameras but also by the quick, single movement of the painter's "developer": "I'm doing like 10,000 lines in one shot, process painting."[44] Whitten's technical innovation remade photography as painting. The mechanical medium was reprocessed from the image *up*—from the distribution of matter already set beneath the titanium ground to the image revealed by the developer in a single stroke. Whitten inverted the photographic process, at least with respect to establishing a foundation for the image in matter before he developed it. In his painting, the development transforms the image; it *becomes* the image. As for the light, it shone from the paint outward as much as passing inward from the environment.

From 1983 on, Whitten's preparation of paint-as-collage sometimes became an exception to his prohibition of brushwork.[45] A quantity of liquid paint could be spread by brush against a surface, allowed to dry, and then lifted and placed on another surface. Whitten was

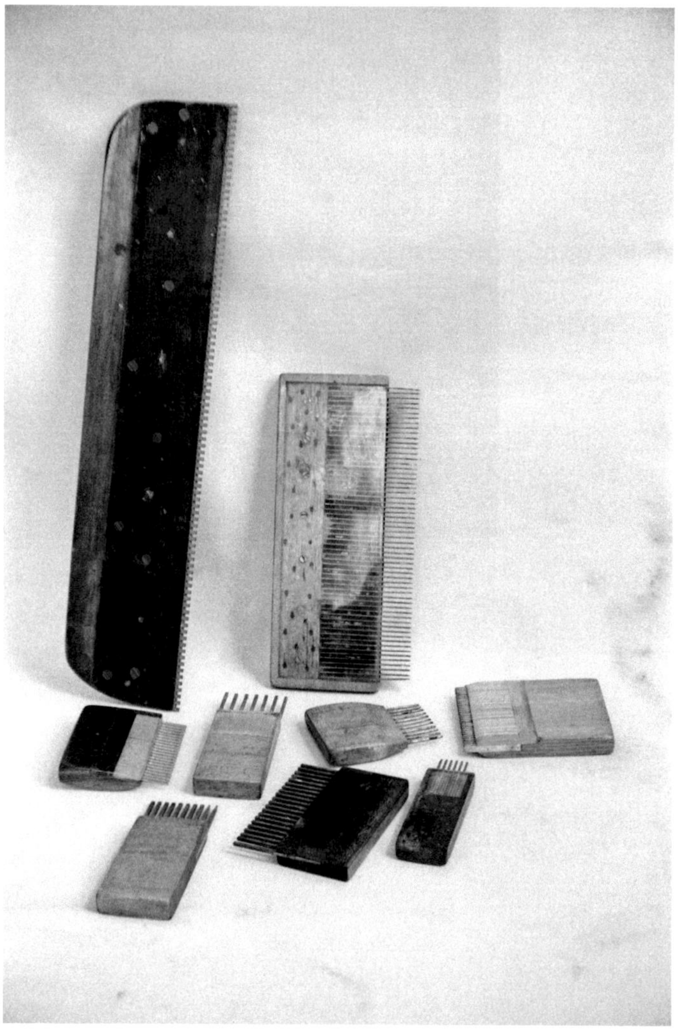

Whitten's photograph, from 1983, of raking (combing) tools

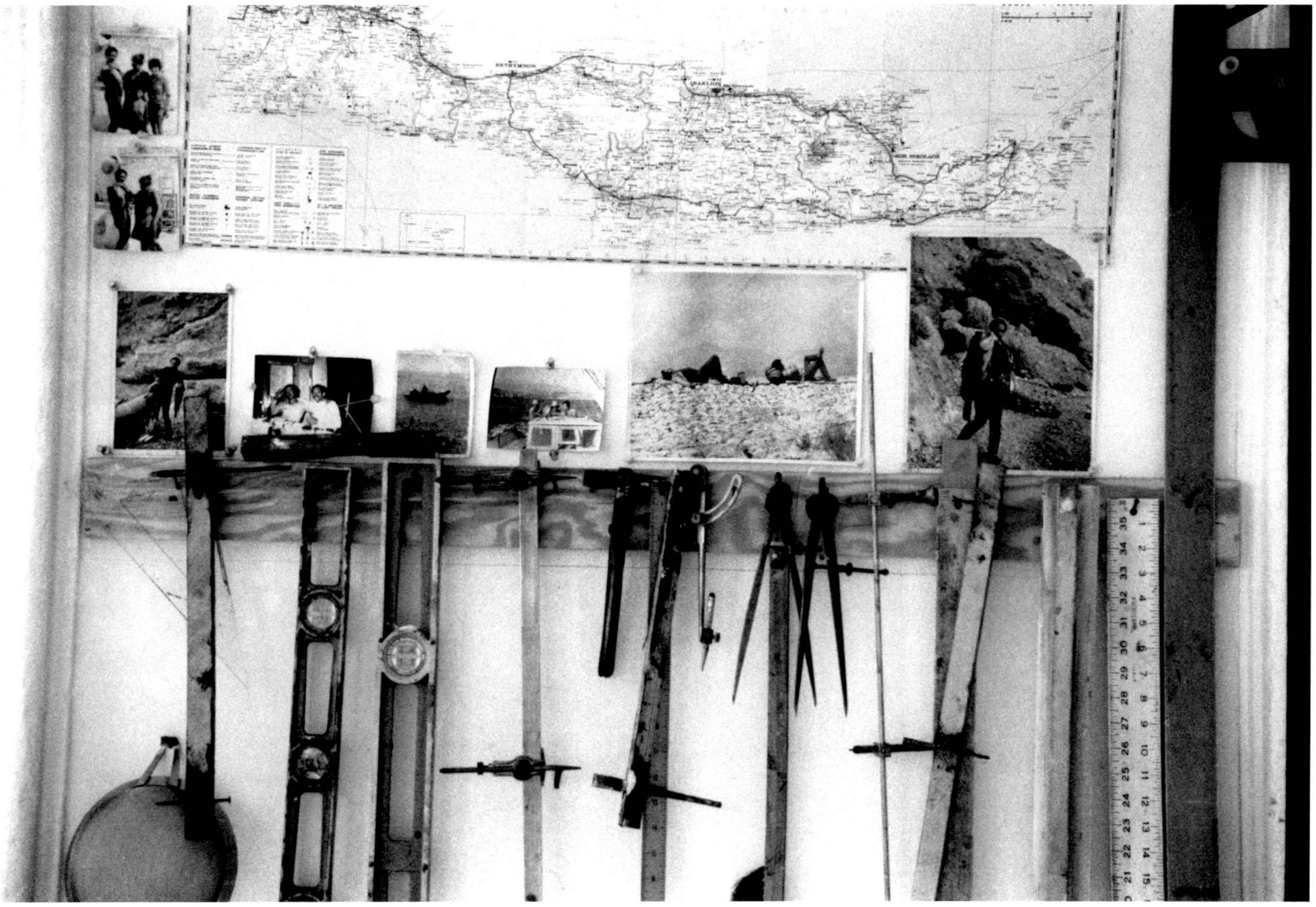

Whitten's photograph of his Lispenard St. studio, 1983

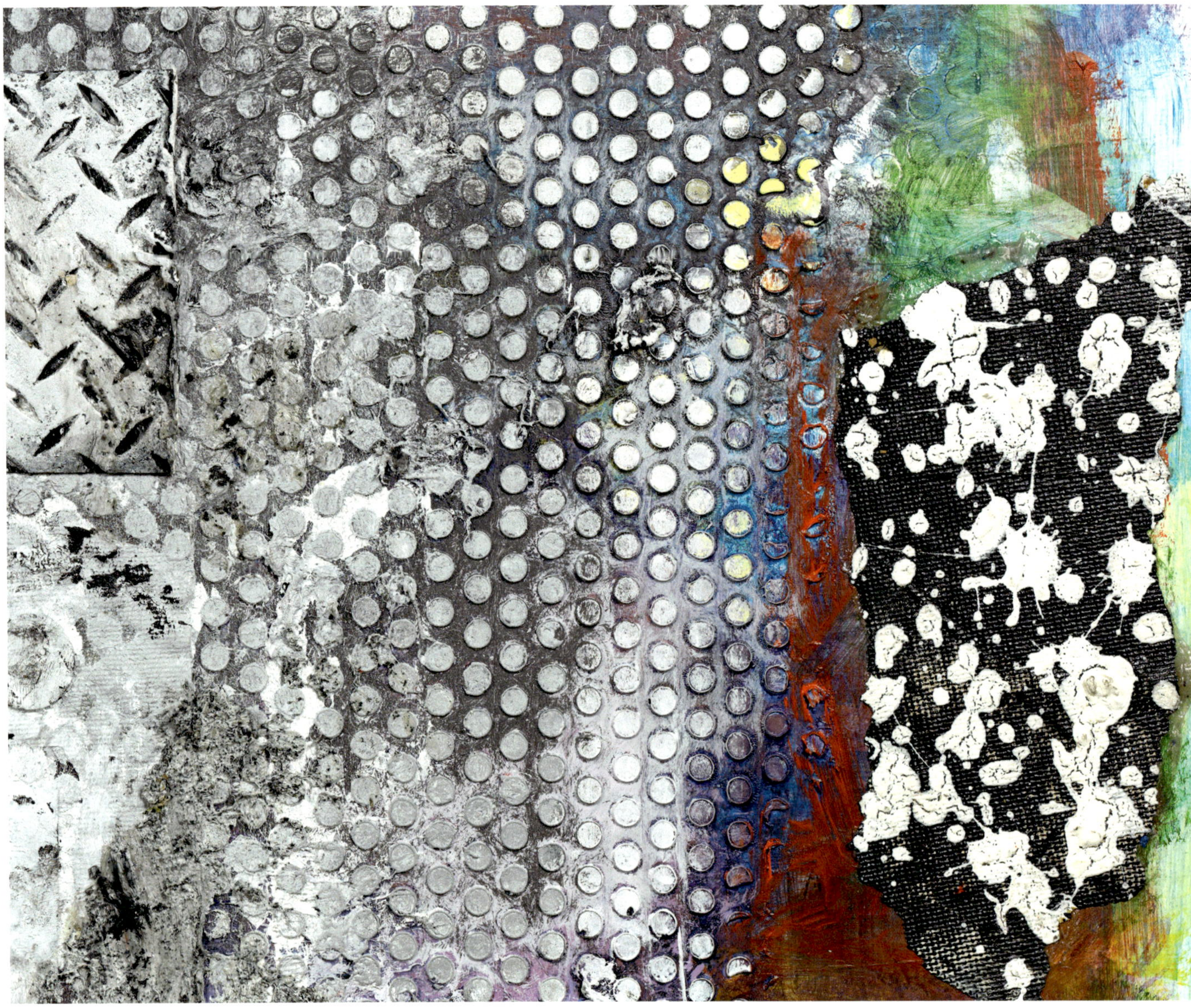

Willi Meets the Keeper (For Willi Smith), 1987, detail

taking advantage of the flexible, plastic properties of acrylic, treating the paint as both malleable and solid, as in *Ode to Andy: For Andy Warhol* (1986 [pp. 73–75]) and *Black Monolith I: A Tribute to James Baldwin* (1988 [p. 85]). By molding and casting elements of imagery for a collage-like painting, he produced the equivalent of differentiated strokes, forms positioned in a series of actions. Each placement was a near-instantaneous gesture. Some of the collaged paint bears a recognizable imprint—bubble wrap in both *Ode to Andy* and *Willi Meets the Keeper (For Willi Smith)* (1987 [above and p. 77])—while other elements appear to be scrap, as in *Site I* (1986 [pp. 27, 67]). Whitten would lift "the paint up off the canvas and then put it back down on the canvas. . . . I'm dealing now [in 1994] with paint as a collage, paint as sculpture. . . . I don't paint a painting, I make a painting."[46] To "paint" was to brush. To "make" was to construct, like laying bricks for a wall, unit by unit. In the case of *Ecdysis I* (1989 [pp. 89, 91]), the large area of collaged white paint was first poured on another surface to assume its shape.[47] One of Whitten's several tributes to Norman Lewis is an exception to more typical procedures (*Norman Lewis Triptych I*, 1985 [pp. 62–65]). Its surface consists of a raised grid of acrylic, the imprint of a screen or grating, over which Whitten added points of oil color; they illuminate the grid selectively, performing a Lewis-like dance across the surface.

In all instances, Whitten's paint became light and matter in one, in service neither to the translation of a preconceived image, nor to any kind of illustration. His paint was the raw material of a building project. "What I want to do," he said in 1998, "is to incorporate 'the image' in 'the matter' on an abstract basis without having to illustrate it. I'm after something which states that 'the painting' is not the illustration of an idea."[48] This had been as true of his purpose in the 1970s and 1980s as in the 1990s. The intervention of conceptualization could be avoided by using a process analogous to photography that benefited from the common belief that the mechanical or electronic nature of a technology renders its imagery objective and without prejudicial perspective. The technologies of vision, both old and new, had no inherent feelings to express, no cultural orientation, save whatever a theory might attribute to them. The same could hardly be said for the "new" hand-painted figuration of the 1980s, with its exaggerated gestures. Yet feeling—sensibility—was at the core of Whitten's contrary art. He would use technology to arrive at an art of felt perception.

THE DNA OF VISUALITY

Before he began to collage fragments of acrylic, Whitten created a series of paintings titled *DNA*, including *DNA XI* (1979 [pp. 36, 38]). He was thinking of the fundamentals of perception, "the DNA of visuality."[49] He later associated DNA with extending art beyond cultural boundaries: "DNA is a molecule shared by all human beings . . . a universal fact in our present society. I apply it to painting because of my belief that painting is organic"—accessible to all human sensibility, to all feeling.[50] Whitten describes his DNA paintings as having "a unified surface that opens to multi-dimensions."[51] Such phrasing defines a raster, whether the mechanical grid used in Renaissance drawing systems or the electronic grid of modern technology. Like light-sensitive photographic film, a pictorial raster awaits its activation, as if differentiated tonalities might be projected from within the surface as much as from without. All points of a raster are of potentially equal value. In his DNA paintings, Whitten imposed material form on a raster already implicit in the orthogonal square of his format. He constructed it—"made" it, rather than "painting" it—by applying a gray slip over a ground previously articulated with imagery of some sort. He then raked the slip in a horizontal direction to create a set of lines that, from above, "developed" the image below. He repeated the process, raking the slip in a vertical direction to complete the grid.[52] Raster and image, process and result, compete for visual attention as one and the same surface.

The optical effect of a DNA painting is strange, to say the least. It puzzled the artist, who did not exhibit the series, but continued to generate variations on the process.[53] The raster lines assume different characters, depending on the composition of the slip and the pressure applied in the raking. Some of the images that shine forth from below are more chromatic than others (*DNA XII*, 1979 [pp. 37, 39]). Some have more clearly articulated form (*DNA X*, 1979 [p. 40]), and some less (*DNA III*, 1979 [p. 41]). In a few closely related works, Whitten imposed paint on the raster lines themselves, so that the image-matter is both below and above (*Confirmation I: Happy Birthday Mary*, 1979 [pp. 45–47]). Elsewhere, the configuration of the raster becomes a kind of weave (*Untitled II*;

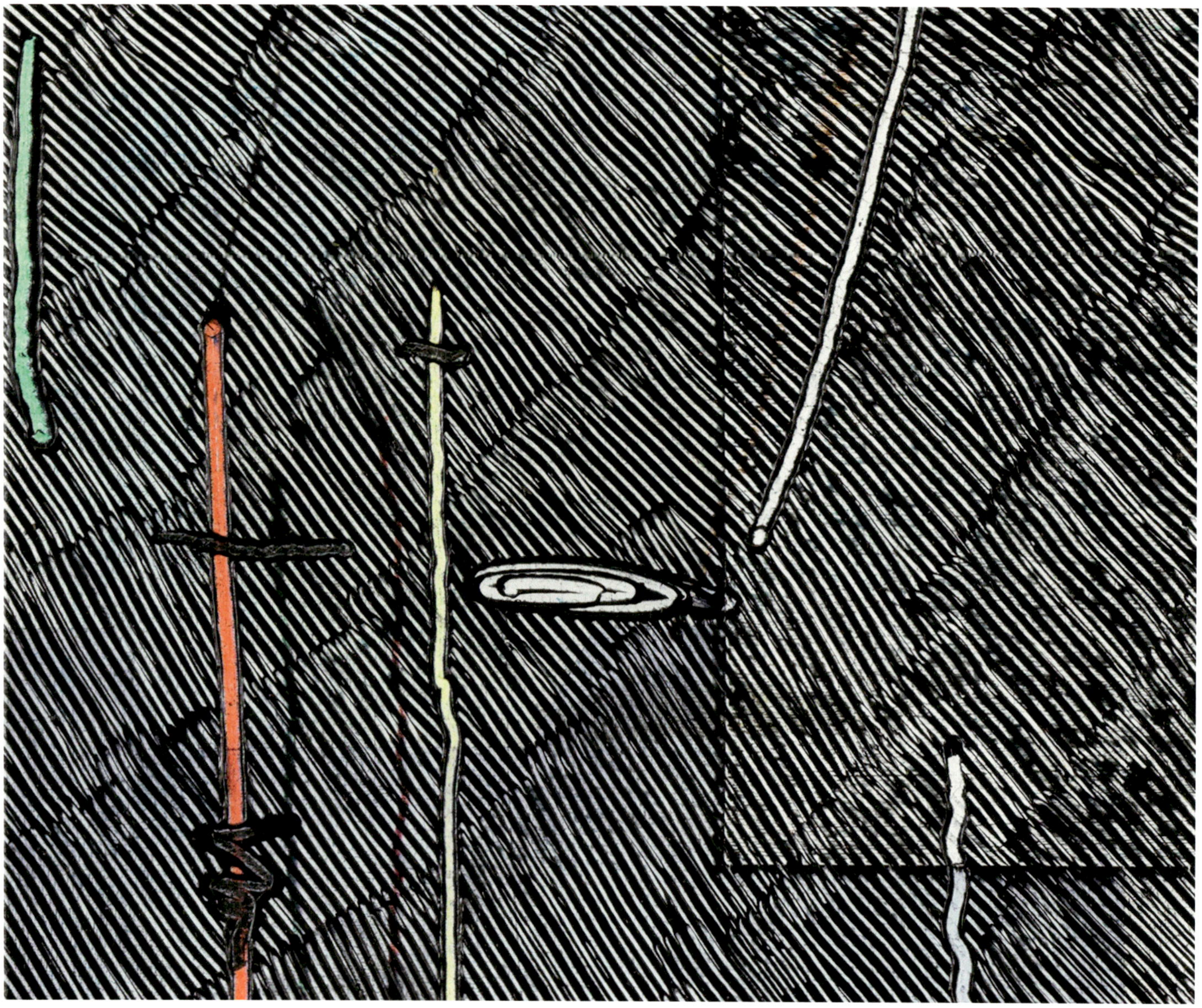

Yellow Cross for Naomi, 1980, detail

Ascension I, 1979 [pp. 32, 35]), or a loosely repetitive pattern (*Yellow Cross for Naomi*, 1980 [above and p. 49]).

In all of these paintings, the perception of the image involves the sense of an inside view (like a feeling emerging, rising to sensation) that in a conventional photographic print would appear as the outside, the raster having remained invisible. By releasing an image in one sweep (*Nee II*) or two (*DNA XI*), or as a collage of elements of equivalent physical presence (*Soweto Disk II AKA Big O for Obama*, 1985; *Site IV*, 1986; *The Burial*, 1989 [p. 87]), Whitten approached the ideal uniformity of a photographic surface, organized by a raster, explicitly or implicitly. He eliminated the marks of expressive hand-gesture and the relational orders of conventional pictorial composition that would give priority to one form over another. In short, he sought the "non-relational": "The crucial part [of the process] took place in three seconds, two seconds. I took Abstract Expressionist gesture and amplified it. That speed removes it from relational thinking to non-relational thinking. Because when that tool I was using [the developer] would fall across the canvas—it did not allow for relational thought."[54] At that instant of development, the composition of the image, whatever it was, was already established by the process. Perhaps Barnett Newman, more than de Kooning or Jackson Pollock (whom Whitten credits), was the true precedent. Only when Newman lifted the masking tape that established his edges, a relatively swift gesture, did the image appear to him (right). Tape was his developer.

Whitten's DNA paintings probed the previous 150 years of photographic technology, during which the dominant representational means of our times evolved in tandem with modern ideological frameworks of thought. He sought the perceptual foundation for what had become such a natural vehicle of visual information that it could be accepted uncritically. His concern was not the imagery of photography, but the working of its mechanism, its process. Recall that Whitten associates speed and a density of information with the contemporary technological environment. His paintings of the 1980s have both, as well as a non-relational character, enhanced by the severe symmetry of some of his formats—often squares or circles. His circular canvases are particularly impressive for their maintenance of appropriately centripetal and centrifugal forces (*Annabelle II*, 1984 [pp. 51–53]; *To My Valentine*, 1984 [p. 55]; *The Kid from Red Bank: The Count*, 1985 [pp. 4, 61]). The distribution of pieces of paint-matter, as well as the precise incisions forming inner rings—executed by a trammel head, an engineering tool used to inscribe arcs, circles, and lines—reiterate the combination of irregular image and regular raster that had characterized the DNA paintings.

Barnett Newman, *Onement II*, 1948. Oil on canvas, 60 x 36 in. (152.4 x 91.4 cm). Wadsworth Atheneum; gift of Jane and Tony Smith, 1967.14

SOUL

As Whitten stated in 1979, "I merely present and dare not explain."[55] He is both romantic and pragmatic, testing his feelings against paint-matter, with intuition alone to guide him. "I'm an American pragmatist," he says, as he seeks "a new type of romanticism . . . which finds comfort in multiple dimensions."[56] Romantics rely on experience. They "become the process"—Whitten's aim.[57]

Leery of logical explanation, Whitten offers analogies. He often alludes to the experience of jazz: "My light in painting is equivalent to [John] Coltrane's sound. . . . I'm speaking in terms of multi-dimensional space. A space that is infinite in all directions."[58] Sound, like light and other wave phenomena, occupies all perceptual dimensions, even time, for nothing limits the distance (of time) that a wave travels. A studio note equates multiple rhythms in music to multiple layers of light in painting: "The density of both depends upon the density of soul."[59] Perhaps soul represents a condensation and compression of waves, as well as their generative source. Whitten perceived dimensions of light as waves that were analogous to Coltrane's "sheets" of sound. By a chain of association, the painter's waves of light passed seamlessly into the "energy fields" that his acrylic matter embodied, as if the material were emitting wave energy of all sorts: not only light and sound, but also electromagnetism and even brain waves that carry both feeling and thought—waves of *soul*. Whitten made a relevant statement when interviewed in 1983 for an exhibition of his work from the 1970s (the type of *Nee II*):

> Coltrane told me how he equated his sound to sheets: the sound you hear in his music comes at you in waves. When they say 'Training [Trane-ing] in,' it's about that sound coming in in waves. He catches it when it comes by . . . I think that, in plastic terms, translating from sound, I was sensing sheets, waves of light. A sheet of light passing, that's how I was seeing light. That's why I refer to these paintings as energy fields. I often thought of them as two poles that create a magnetic field in which light is trapped.[60]

Light is the cause of what we see. More than the medium of vision, light is vision's soul.

Whitten's experience of the Manhattan jazz scene reinforced his vivid sense that music, like painting, elicits the presence of soul. The connection of music or song to soul also has a classic source in black literature, W. E. B. Du Bois's *The Souls of Black Folk*, which Whitten recalls from his student years.[61] Du Bois argued that song—specifically, the so-called Negro spirituals—captures a range of thoughts and feelings that affect the human soul, not just the black soul but every soul. Song bridges the divide between the races as well as the separation of individuals. Du Bois promoted the humanizing effect of song, its soul: "Sometime, somewhere, men will judge men by their souls and not by their skins."[62]

One way to conceive of soul—invoking Whitten's language—is to regard it as the "molecular" form of both thinking and feeling: emotional feeling and rational thinking as a molecular unit, before ideological and cultural forces induce the human faculties to diverge and conflict, diminishing empathy. Whitten regards the molecular unit, which he also designates as DNA, as the "door to perception . . . the sheer act of perceiving."[63] Soul is multi-dimensional, as is perception. Through the decades, Whitten has been attempting to catch it in paint, to contain it like Coltrane's wave: "Painting . . . is a soul space!"[64] He recalls Du Bois's concept of the Veil that conceals African American life within American society.[65] An art of soul, exposing viewers to perception in its molecular form, its shared universality, has the effect of removing the Veil and all other ideological barriers. Here aesthetic innovation becomes a social benefit.

EVERSION

Consider a hypothesis. If a single principle characterizes Whitten's art of the decade 1979–1989, it might be this: he was engaged with indexical processes in the absence of iconic forms to guide them to a proper, expected end. His various processes involve complex ways of layering paint, incising paint (*Black in Time I*, 1980 [p. 48]), molding paint, and collaging paint. For each process, the product was the process itself—an index playing the role of icon, or, to push the issue to an extreme, an index lacking any corresponding icon whatsoever (like a photographic process without a photographic print to show for it).

Invoking the concepts of index and icon may cause the issue to become too intellectual and less amenable to feeling, let alone soul. To put it less abstractly: Whitten's art constituted a form of photography—etymologically, drawing with light—but with manually prepared paint replacing light-sensitive chemicals or a grid of electronic sensors. Arranging molecules of perception as paint-matter, in advance of developing an immaterial image of light, Whitten inverted the photographic process. No matter which variant of the technology we consider—the irregular distribution of emulsion in analog photography, the regular grid of half-tone printing, the ordered raster in both video and digital photography—Whitten's process is the more proactive. An image does not appear passively as the result of his technical operation; rather, the process acts as the image.[66]

A photographic lens focuses light, and the light imprints an image on a photosensitive surface. Whitten's paintings project light outward, not inward: "It was something about seeing light come through from underneath outward."[67] He observed this phenomenon in his work of the 1970s—as much a wonder to him as to others. We commonly think that an artist has an idea, concept, or "vision," with the work of art designed to represent it. But Whitten thought of the source of his image as his materials, not himself: "The image comes from the material. . . . Painting is the medium not me. . . . It must be able to exist outside of the self."[68] He perceives a parallel in the Byzantine notion of acheiropoietic marking, in which an image makes itself without the guide of an artist's hands.[69] As of 1970, Whitten's paint became cause and effect in one.

A work completed in December 1988, *The Alliance* (pp. 78–79), is a horizontal that fails to act like one. Its ground consists of acrylic casts of various patterned surfaces; because the patterns repeat up and down and left and right, the horizontal rectangle performs as if it were more symmetrical than it is. In a studio log written at the time, Whitten made a comment similar to the one quoted at the beginning of this essay (recorded about a year later), in which he invokes sensibility: "The political significance of what I am doing depends upon my ability to project beyond art history. The so-called mainstream must be bent, deflected and detoured in a direction dictated by the profundity of my sensibility. *The Alliance* . . . offers such a detour. *The Alliance* is a pact conceived of as a marriage of necessity between matter and spirit."[70] For "spirit," we can substitute "soul." Whitten also wrote: "I do not accept the separation of spirit from matter."[71]

Whitten's "alliance" of matter and spirit began in 1964. At that time, he made a number of small works with canvas as a support, to which he applied fluid black and white acrylic; over this, he stretched tulle netting, allowing the paint to seep through. When he wiped away the excess, the remaining images resembled "blurred photographs," as in *Head III*, 1964 (p. 26).[72] Ghostly images emerged from underneath.[73] Their soft focus resembled that of the images that would appear in the DNA paintings of 1979, but they lacked the interference of an overriding grid (because the weave of the tulle was very fine). Concerning 1964 and photography, Whitten recalls: "It was the invention of photography that changed our perception in painting. It gave us a freedom that we never had before. . . . Those gray paintings were fantastic, but I didn't understand them." This was the moment of the notorious statement that haunted Whitten more persistently

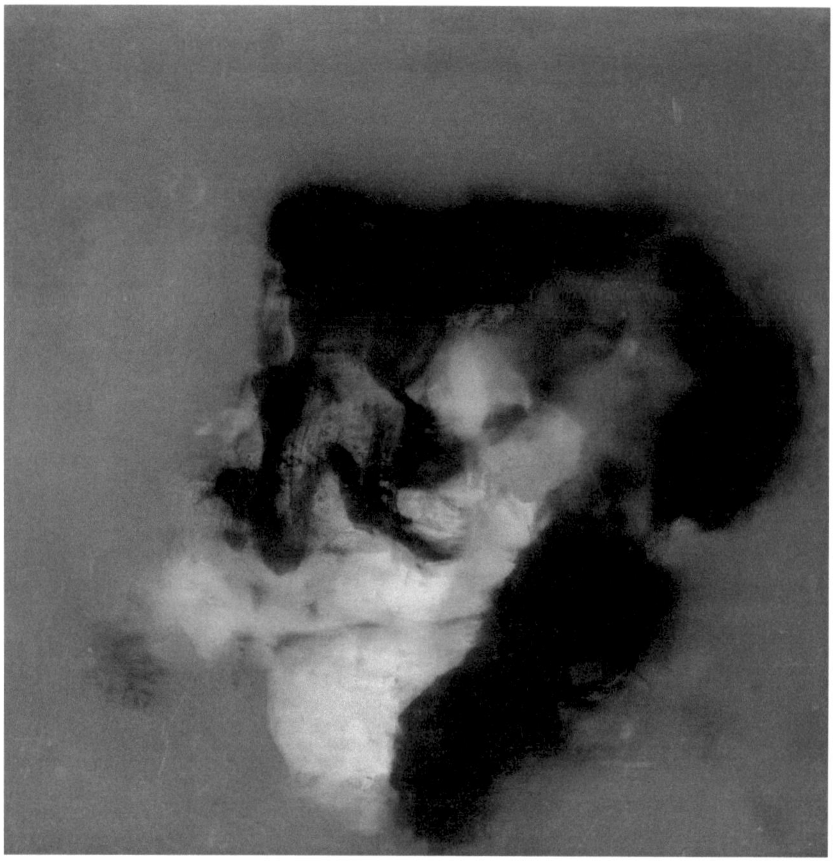

Head III, 1964. Acrylic on canvas, 15 x 16 in. (38.1 x 40.6 cm)

than his blurry "ghosts": "The image is photographic. Therefore, I must photograph my thoughts."[74]

Now, the promised speculation. There are numerous studio notes from the 1980s that seem to dovetail with Whitten's cryptic logic of 1964. Among them, two seem particularly germane with regard to his conception of photographic process. First, a note from 1986, the time of *Site I* and *Site IV*: "If we extend the meaning of the painting as object (to include the immaterial), that object in its material form could very well become spirit. Light functions as the element which dematerializes the object and allows it to become spirit."[75] We should recall that Whitten's paintings, essentially works in low relief, capture and reflect light more actively than do flat surfaces. Second, a note dated a year later, 1987: "I want a picture of the other side. A mental photograph of the psyche."[76] This notion evokes the psychological distress that Whitten experienced in 1964, as a result of his obsessive desire to "photograph [his] thoughts": "I sincerely thought that I was a camera. . . . I'd see things on the street, and I'd go click, click, click."[77] In 1987, however, the same camera points to "the other side." It focuses inwardly on thought as spirit—"a mental photograph of the psyche"—rather than outwardly on thought as vision. This reorientation of the photographic process, conducted in painting, is more than an inversion. It should be regarded as an eversion: a turn inside out, an overturning, a revolution.

Whitten's revelation—"The image is photographic. Therefore, I must photograph my thoughts"—refers to a shift from picture-making to process-making. It did

Site I, 1986

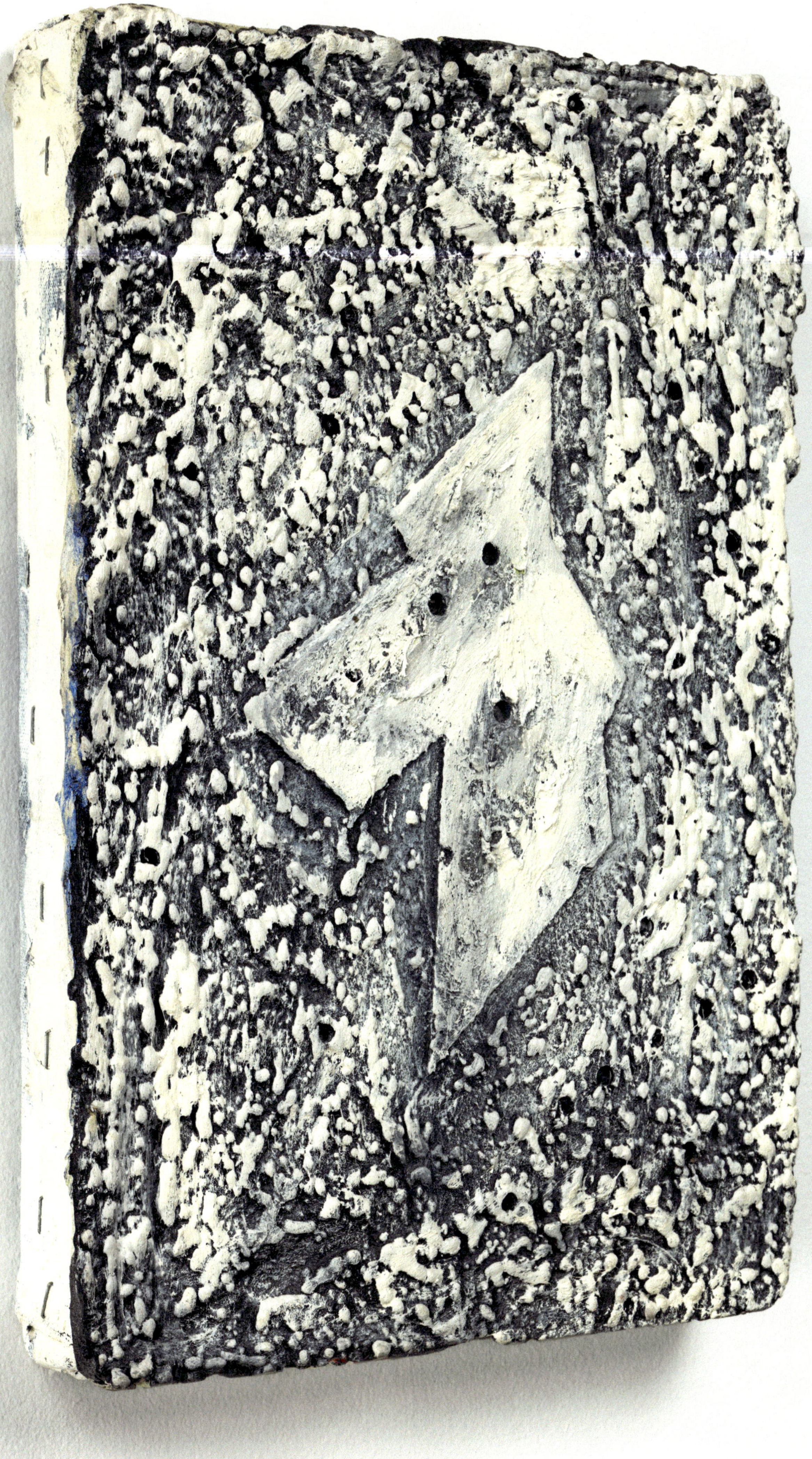

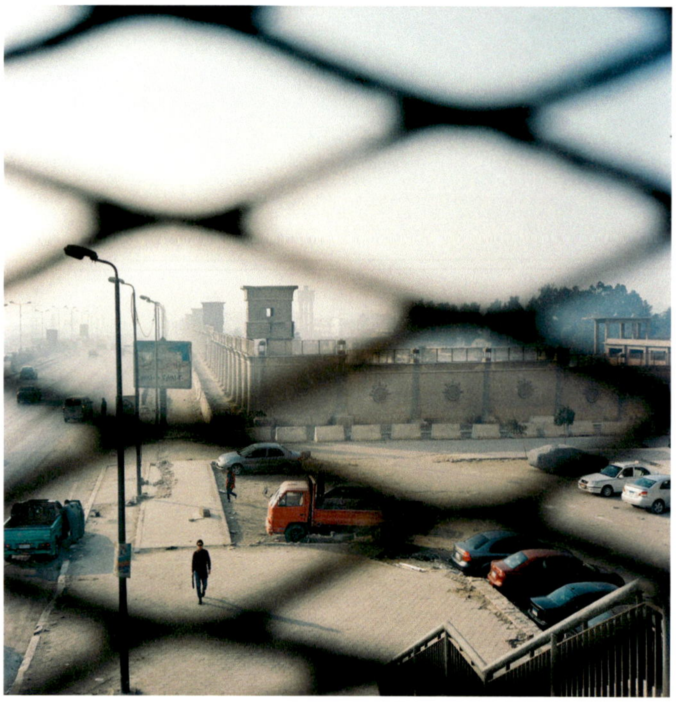

Tora Prison, Cairo, Egypt

not become his definitive practice until the 1970s. Photography, whether inverted or everted, was the technological model. Whitten's art sets a materialized raster at the outer layer of an image-bearing surface, like a window to the soul. The raster or grid is a process-element, an index that leaves an image as its iconic trace. But what we see is the process itself (imprinting, casting, and so forth). And if we were to see into "the other side" with our photographic painting process, we would be observing inner thoughts, the faculty of imagination, which itself ought to be generating images. We would expose a psychic process to a technological process—mind recorded in matter. I wonder if Whitten was approaching some notion of this sort when he composed another note of 1986 (quoted above, but in abbreviated form): "Painting . . . exists somewhere between knowing and not knowing. . . . It's about us, about what we are not, what we are. It's a soul space!"[78]

A few months ago, as I was beginning to formulate thoughts about an essay on Jack Whitten's art, with emphasis on the period 1979–1989, I puzzled over the small DNA paintings of 1979, to which I was immediately attracted. Lacking words to articulate the feeling, I nevertheless intuited that Whitten had—with paint—turned my sense of photography inside out. Soon afterward, a chance encounter with a photograph from a news magazine confirmed this understanding (left). The photographer's mission was to depict Tora Prison, outside Cairo, Egypt. Perhaps because no better position could be reached, the exposure was taken through a screen of fencing, an open grid of diagonals. With the focus set to the distance of the prison, the fencing blurs, due to its proximity to the lens of the camera. Grids are neutral, non-relational rasters; they aid in stabilizing the relational elements of a composition (in this instance, a receding roadway, an adjacent building, a foreground parking area and walkway). But if conceived as a raster, the diagonal grid of the prison photograph becomes dysfunctional. Its units are too large, and their edges seem to spread in soft focus, lacking precision. A proper raster assumes little more than a virtual presence; it orders a situation and retreats from the scene, like a penciled grid used to guide the perspective of a painted landscape. Here, the repetitive pattern appears to signify a material object rather than a graphic system. It obstructs the view. Yet this was the position from which the prison could best be photographed. The photographer merely responded to live conditions.[79]

In any event, the fencing, situated within the view to be pictured, could not simultaneously have been functioning as a raster for the photographic apparatus. But it strongly evokes one—everted. As I viewed this image, the diagonal grid became the subject of the picture. I could perceive it no other way. Was this everted order evident only because I had already seen Whitten's *DNA XI*? In fact, much of my description of the prison photograph would serve *DNA XI* reasonably well. In the canvas, I found myself drawn to the surface of horizontal and vertical "developer" lines—grainy, like the diagonals in the photograph—each set of delineations a raster of sorts.[80]

Yet, there is the *light*. Whitten's material raster, silvery with additions of silica and graphite, projects a surface light along with the illumination coming from underneath—altogether, a multi-dimensional light. The prison photograph is engaging, but its light is limited. *DNA XI* is of a different order of sensation. It has the soul of painting.

Notes

1 Jack Whitten, statement in Smithsonian Archives of American Art, "Oral History with Jack Whitten, 2009, December 1–3" (interview by Judith Olch Richards), at https://www.aaa.si.edu/collections/interviews/oral-history-interview-jack-whitten-15748, accessed July 14, 2017. I am immensely grateful to Jack Whitten, Mary Staikos (Whitten), and Mirsini Whitten Amidon for numerous conversations, studio visits, and aid in acquiring documentation. The generosity of the Whitten family is without bounds. I thank Jeannie McKetta and Gilles Heno-Coe for essential assistance in research.

2 Whitten, studio note, November 11, 1989 (emphasis eliminated). Jack Whitten and Mirsini Whitten Amidon offered access to the artist's studio notes dated 1979 to 1989. In quoting from these casual notes, I have occasionally regularized orthography and syntax, careful not to alter the sense of the statement.

3 Whitten, studio note, "Battle Plan," fall 1983.

4 Whitten, "Notes on DNA Paintings," unpublished text, February 2017. This and other unpublished texts quoted in this essay are courtesy Jack Whitten.

5 Whitten, studio note, November 4, 1979 (emphasis original).

6 Ibid.

7 Whitten, "Perspectives at the Blanton: Jack Whitten and Kellie Jones," Blanton Museum of Art, Austin, Texas, February 22, 2015; "Jack Whitten: 101," unpublished text, April 2015; "Door to the River," unpublished text, May 2015.

8 Whitten, interview by Cristina Scorza, Museum of Contemporary Art San Diego, September 7, 2014, in *Jack Whitten: Five Decades of Painting*, ed. Kathryn Kanjo (San Diego: Museum of Contemporary Art, 2015), 19.

9 Whitten, email to the author, June 9, 2016.

10 Whitten, in Robert Storr, "In Conversation with Jack Whitten," *Jack Whitten: Five Decades of Painting*, 55. Whitten has referred to the statement about photography in a number of interviews, on occasion dating it 1965; but 1964 seems to be definitive.

11 Whitten, in conversation with the author, March 30, 2017. To this point, Michelle Kuo writes: "Instead of showing or talking about subject matter, Whitten engages the very instruments that would prove most adept at controlling content and shaping subjects": Michelle Kuo, statement accompanying "Jack Whitten: A Portfolio," *Artforum* 50 (February 2012): 195.

12 Whitten, in conversation with the author, June 4, 2017.

13 Whitten, studio note, April 9, 1988.

14 Whitten, interview by Stuart Horodner, November 2, 2007, quoted in Stuart Horodner, "Jack Whitten: Memory and Method," *Jack Whitten: Memorial Paintings* (Atlanta: Atlanta Contemporary Art Center, 2008), 13.

15 Whitten, in conversation with the author, June 4, 2017.

16 Whitten, Smithsonian Archives of American Art, "Oral History with Jack Whitten, 2009, December 1–3."

17 Whitten, in conversation with the author, July 12, 2017.

18 Whitten, studio note, November 4, 1979 (emphasis original).

19 Whitten, "Jack Whitten: An African-American and Pollock" (interview by Jeanne Siegel), in Jeanne Siegel, *Painting After Pollock: Structures of Influence* (Amsterdam: G+B Arts International, 1999), 144.

20 Whitten wrote recently: "Sincerity, authenticity, and substance are classical elements of painting's historical legacy, and are not to be taken lightly as stylistic devices manipulated by fashionable 'art aficionados'"; Whitten, "Beyond Abstraction," unpublished text, September 2015.

21 Ludwig Wittgenstein, *Tractatus Logico-Philosophicus*, trans. D. F. Pears and B. F. McGuinness (London: Routledge & Kegan Paul, 1961 [1921]); Jacques Derrida, *Of Grammatology*, trans. Gayatri Chakravorty Spivak (Baltimore: The Johns Hopkins University Press, 1974 [1967]).

22 Douglas Crimp, "The Photographic Activity of Postmodernism," *October* 15 (winter 1980): 91. On distinguishing originality from innovation, see Richard Shiff, "Original Copy," *Common Knowledge* 3 (spring 1994): 88–107.

23 Whitten, studio note, February 12, 1979 (emphasis added). Or, alternatively, a later variation on the theme of historical liberation: "The history of painting has freed me from the past. . . . The scene is clean"; Whitten, email to the author, July 25, 2017.

24 Whitten, studio note, February 12, 1979.

25 Whitten, "Jack Whitten: An African-American and Pollock," *Painting After Pollock*, 135.

26 Ibid., 139–40.

27 Ibid., 140.

28 Whitten, studio note, April 27, 1987.

29 Whitten, studio note, February 12, 1979.

30 Whitten, interview by Henry Geldzahler, March 31, 1983, quoted in Henry Geldzahler, *Jack Whitten: Ten Years—1970–1980* (New York: Studio Museum in Harlem, 1983), 8; "Beyond Abstraction," unpublished text, September 2015.

31 Whitten, "Beyond Abstraction," unpublished text, September 2015.

32 Whitten, in conversation with the author, June 4, 2017.

33 Whitten, in conversation with the author, March 30, 2017. My reference is to Charles Sanders Peirce; Whitten's is to Edmund Husserl. The indexical and the eidetic are hardly the same, but they share a number of perceptual effects.

34 Whitten, in conversation with the author, June 4, 2017.

35 Whitten, statement in Kenneth Goldsmith, "Jack Whitten," *Bomb* 48 (summer 1994) at http://bombmagzine.org/article/1772;jack-whitten, accessed July 16, 2017.

36 Ibid.

37 A prominent critic argued in 1981 that most contemporary work in painting "confirms the hieratics of ideological domination"; Benjamin H. D. Buchloh, "Figures of Authority, Ciphers of Regression: Notes on the Return of Representation in European Painting" (1981), in Brian Wallis, ed., *Art After Modernism: Rethinking Representation* (New York: The New Museum of Contemporary Art, 1984), 124. All painting was authoritarian by default, since this was the dominant institutionalized medium of representation during periods of authoritarian political order. Damned by association, any artist who persisted in painting during the 1980s was regarded as having assumed the pose of an authority figure. The exception would be painters working only to discredit painting. Supposedly, such negativity constituted an advance in ideological awareness.

38 Whitten, "Closing the Gap between Painting and Sculpture," unpublished text, October 2016.

39 See Todd Gustavson, *Camera: A History of Photography from Daguerreotype to Digital* (New York: Sterling, 2009), 340.

40 Whitten, in Storr, "In Conversation with Jack Whitten," *Jack Whitten: Five Decades of Painting*, 55; "In Conversation: Jack Whitten with Robert Storr," *Brooklyn Rail*, September 2007, at http://brooklynrail.org/2007/9/art/whitten, accessed July 16, 2017.

41 Whitten, "In Conversation: Jack Whitten with Jarrett Earnest," *Brooklyn Rail*, February 2017, at http://brooklynrail.org/2017/02/art/JACK-WHITTEN-with-Jarrett-Earnest, accessed February 21, 2017.

42 Whitten, in conversation with the author, February 12, 2017.

43 Whitten, "Door to the River," unpublished text, May 2015.

44 Whitten, Smithsonian Archives of American Art, "Oral History with Jack Whitten, 2009, December 1–3."

45 Whitten lost approximately three years of work between the time of a building fire in March 1980 and early 1983. The hiatus led to a shift in his practice, from works involving a "developer" to those making use of molds and casts.

46 Whitten, in Goldsmith, "Jack Whitten."

47 Whitten, email to the author, July 25, 2017.

48 Whitten, "Jack Whitten: An African-American and Pollock," *Painting After Pollock*, 135.

49 Whitten, studio note, November 4, 1979. In 1983, Whitten related the fundamental core of visual perception, its DNA, to an understanding he derived from viewing the geometric order of African sculpture as well as the structure of brushstrokes in the art of Cézanne; Whitten, in Geldzahler, *Jack Whitten: Ten Years—1970–1980*, 8. In 1984, he pursued the same topic: "There's a grid under [African wood carving], a molecular structure that explains how the artist perceives things. . . . The sculpture [made] me aware of the molecular physicality of painting, or paint as matter": Whitten, statement, June 4, 1984, in The Center Gallery of Bucknell University, *Since the Harlem Renaissance: 50 Years of Afro-American Art* (Lewisburg: Center Gallery of Bucknell University, 1984), 43.

50 Whitten, "Notes on DNA Paintings," unpublished text, February 2017.

51 Whitten, in conversation with the author, May 7, 2017.

52 "The first layer of acrylic slip is left to dry and then another vertical planar sweep is applied and left to dry, creating an optical grid pattern strictly through process": Whitten, "Notes on DNA Paintings," unpublished text, February 2017.

53 Whitten, in conversation with the author, July 12, 2017.

54 Whitten, in Goldsmith, "Jack Whitten." Whitten's initial realization that he could work in a non-relational manner came when he created "the Slab", a multi-layered body of acrylic that could be manipulated as matter in various ways, in 1970; Whitten, "Jack Whitten: An African-American and Pollock," *Painting After Pollock*, 131. He refers to the Slab as a "line" because a single directional movement forms it; its material substance converts the mental concept of line to obdurate matter; Whitten, in conversation with the author, January 25, 2017.

55 Whitten, studio note, February 12, 1979.

56 Whitten, "In Conversation: Jack Whitten with Jarrett Earnest"; "Closing the Gap Between Painting and Sculpture," unpublished text, October 2016.

57 Whitten, in conversation with the author, July 12, 2017.

58 Whitten, in Goldsmith, "Jack Whitten."

59 Whitten, studio note, January 25, 1988.

60 Whitten, in Geldzahler, *Jack Whitten: Ten Years—1970–1980*, 8. See also Whitten, in Storr, "In Conversation with Jack Whitten," *Jack Whitten: Five Decades of Painting*, 53. Whitten had played tenor saxophone with jazz groups, and knew Coltrane during the 1960s (Whitten, in conversation with the author, July 12, 2017). The phrase "sheets of sound" appeared in 1958 in liner notes by critic Ira Gitler for the Coltrane album *Soultrane*.

61 Whitten, in conversation with the author, May 7, 2017.

62 W. E. B. Du Bois, *The Souls of Black Folk* (eBook: Start Publishing, 2012 [1903]), 246.

63 Whitten, in conversation with the author, May 7, 2017. He dates his use of the term "molecular perception" to 1979; Whitten, Smithsonian Archives of American Art, "Oral History with Jack Whitten, 2009, December 1–3."

64 Whitten, studio note, January 6, 1986.

65 Du Bois, *The Souls of Black Folk*, 9–10.

66 One of Whitten's studio notes (January 31, 1983) approaches this notion: "That light [in my painting] must define a space, not a pictorial space. A space which is actually the image."

67 Whitten, in Storr, "In Conversation with Jack Whitten," *Jack Whitten: Five Decades of Painting*, 57.

68 Whitten, studio notes, April 9, 1988; February 12, 1979; March 22, 1987. See also the note of February 15, 1986: "We must go beyond the self, to get rid of the me."

69 Whitten, in conversation with the author, January 25, 2017.

70 Whitten, studio note, December 10, 1988.

71 Whitten, studio note, January 20, 1990.

72 Whitten, in Storr, "In Conversation with Jack Whitten," *Jack Whitten: Five Decades of Painting*, 55.

73 Michelle Kuo referred to the "ghosted movement" of the gray paintings, which recalled "spirit photography and infrared video alike"; Kuo, statement accompanying "Jack Whitten: A Portfolio," 195. Kathryn Kanjo noted their "ghostly impressions"; Kathryn Kanjo, "Facing Abstraction," *Jack Whitten: Five Decades of Painting*, 21.

74 Whitten, in Storr, "In Conversation with Jack Whitten," *Jack Whitten: Five Decades of Painting*, 55.

75 Whitten, studio note, March 19, 1986 (emphasis eliminated).

76 Whitten, studio note, March 8, 1987.

77 Whitten, in Storr, "In Conversation with Jack Whitten," *Jack Whitten: Five Decades of Painting*, 55.

78 Whitten, studio note, January 6, 1986.

79 The possibility remains that the photographer intended the screen of fencing as a metaphor for imprisonment; but this was never my impression, perhaps due to the influence of analogous examples of Whitten's art.

80 At a distance, these forms become more apparent, as if the photographic process were bringing them into focus, just as the supervening raster passes out of focus. Whitten's paintings are dynamic.

PLATES

Ascension I, 1979

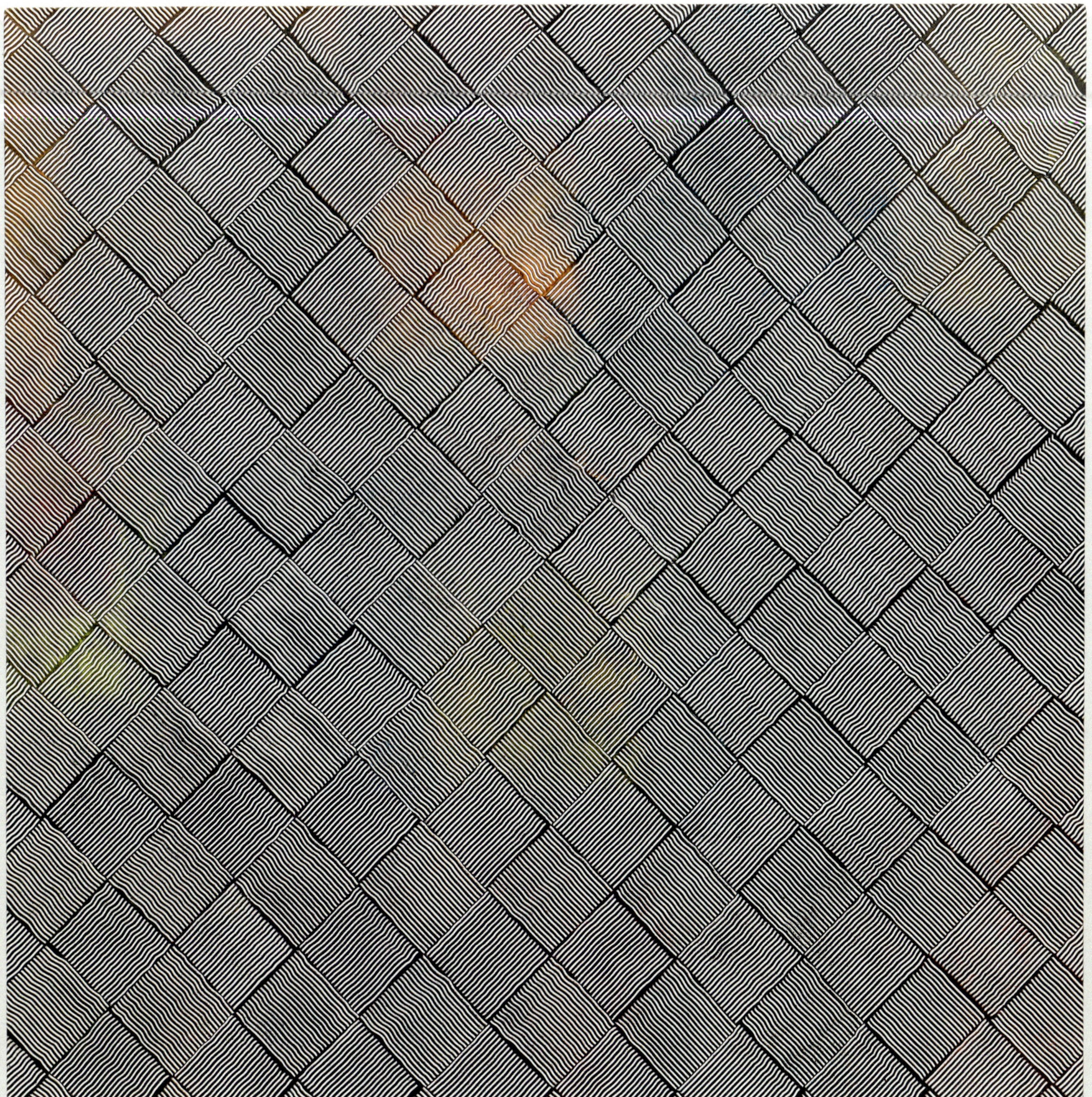

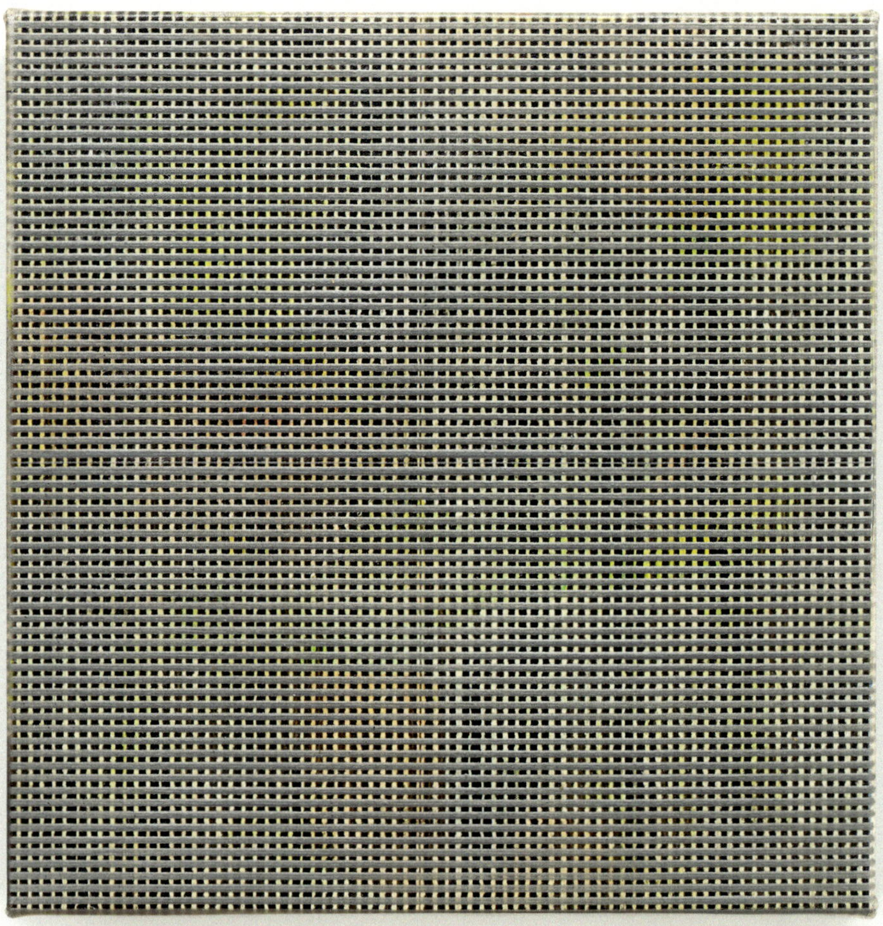

DNA XI, 1979

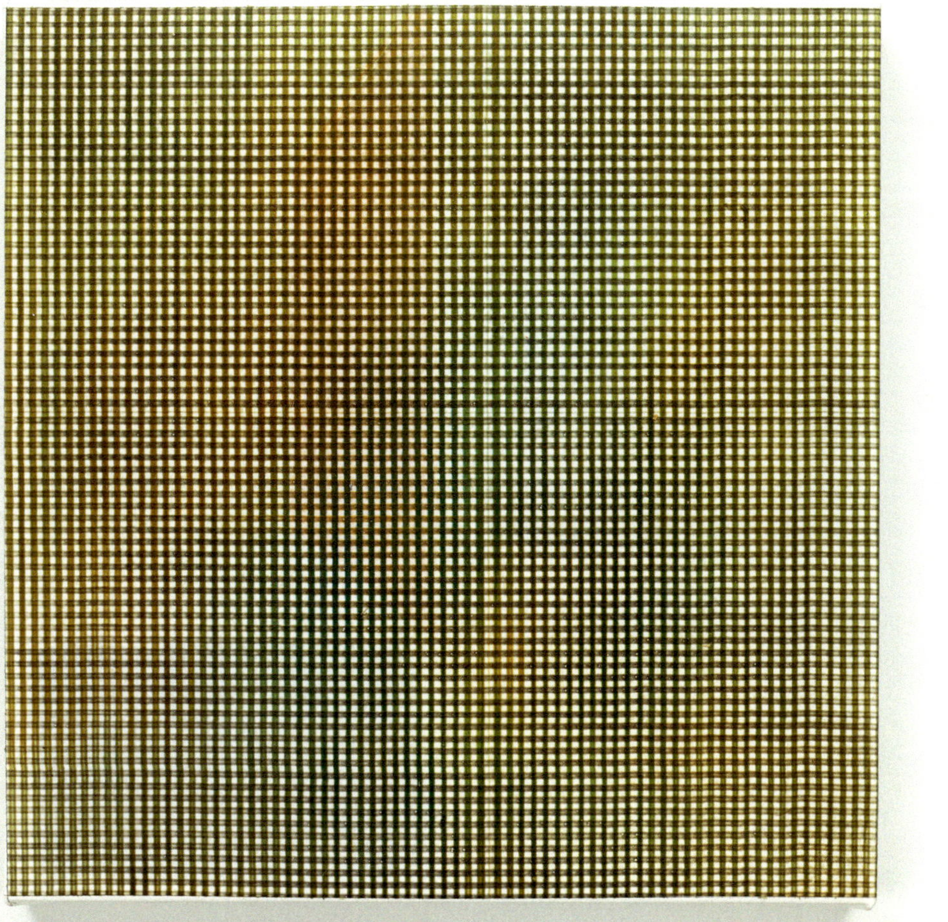

DNA XII, 1979

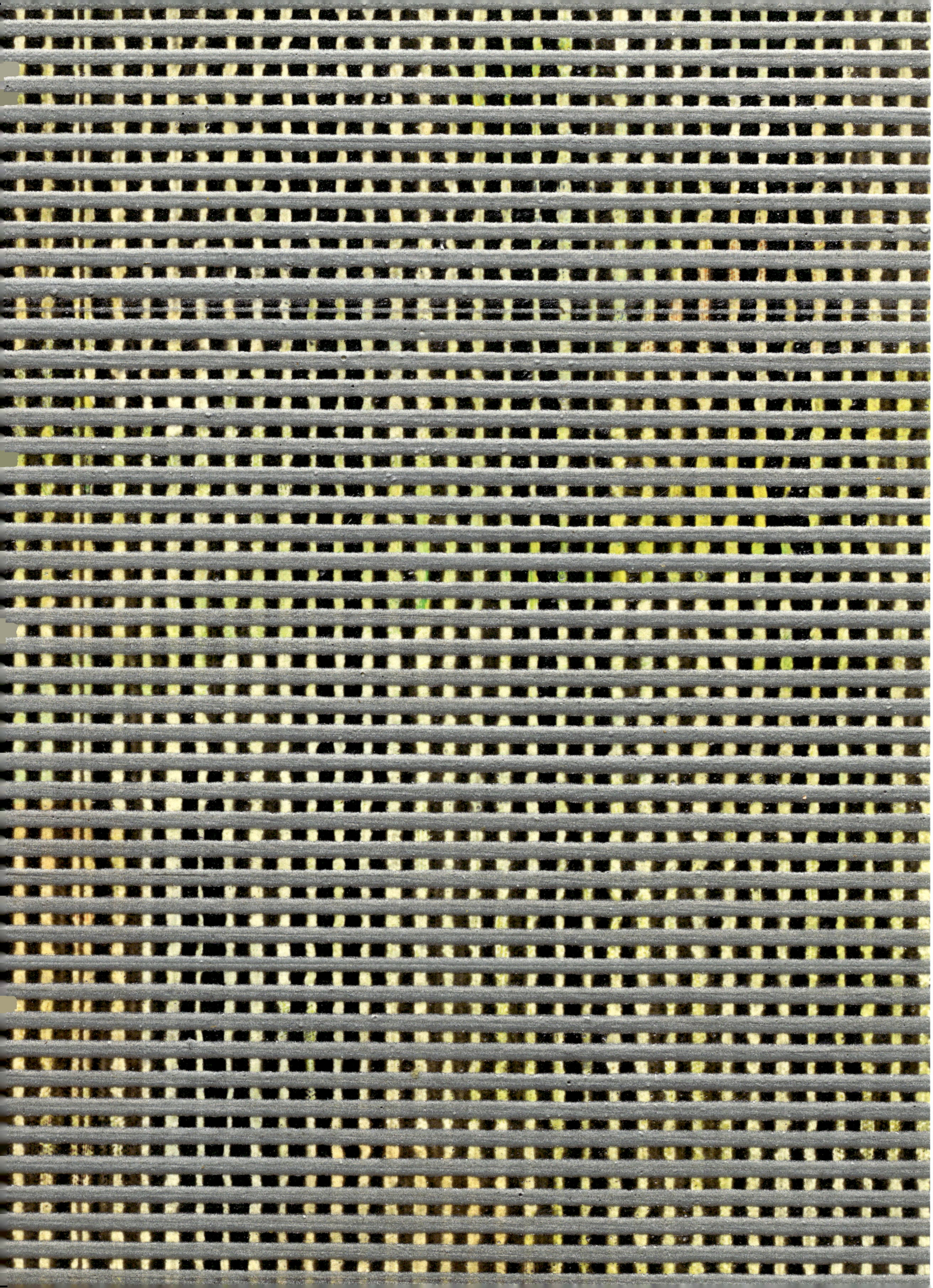

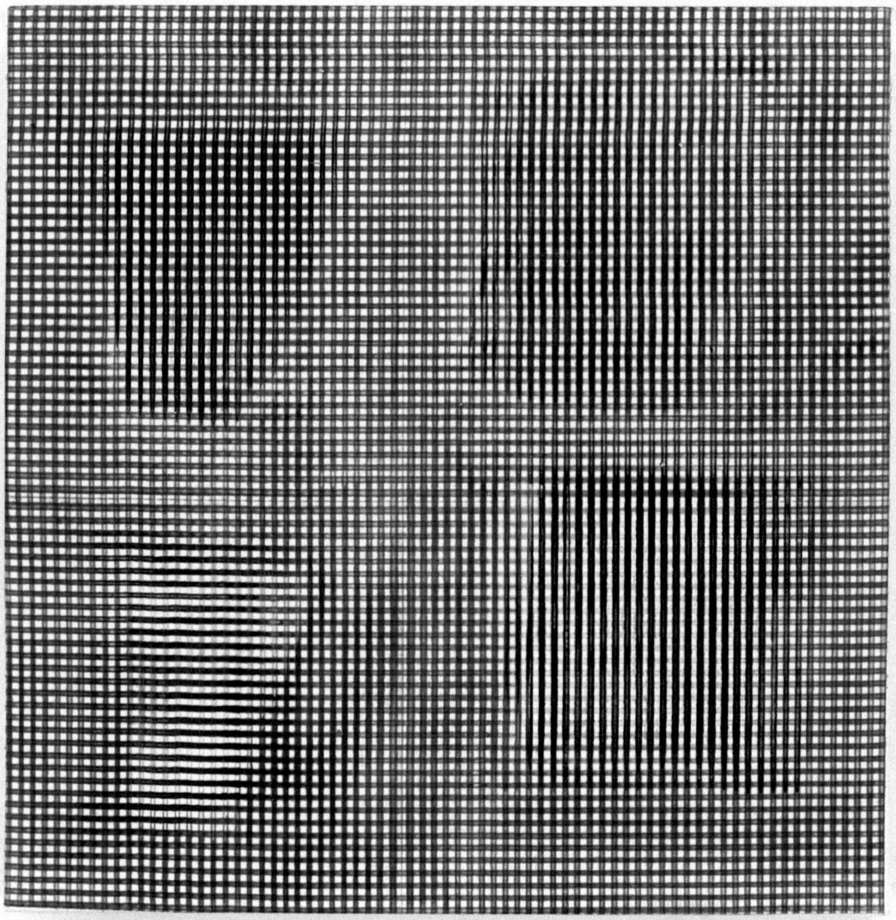

DNA X, 1979

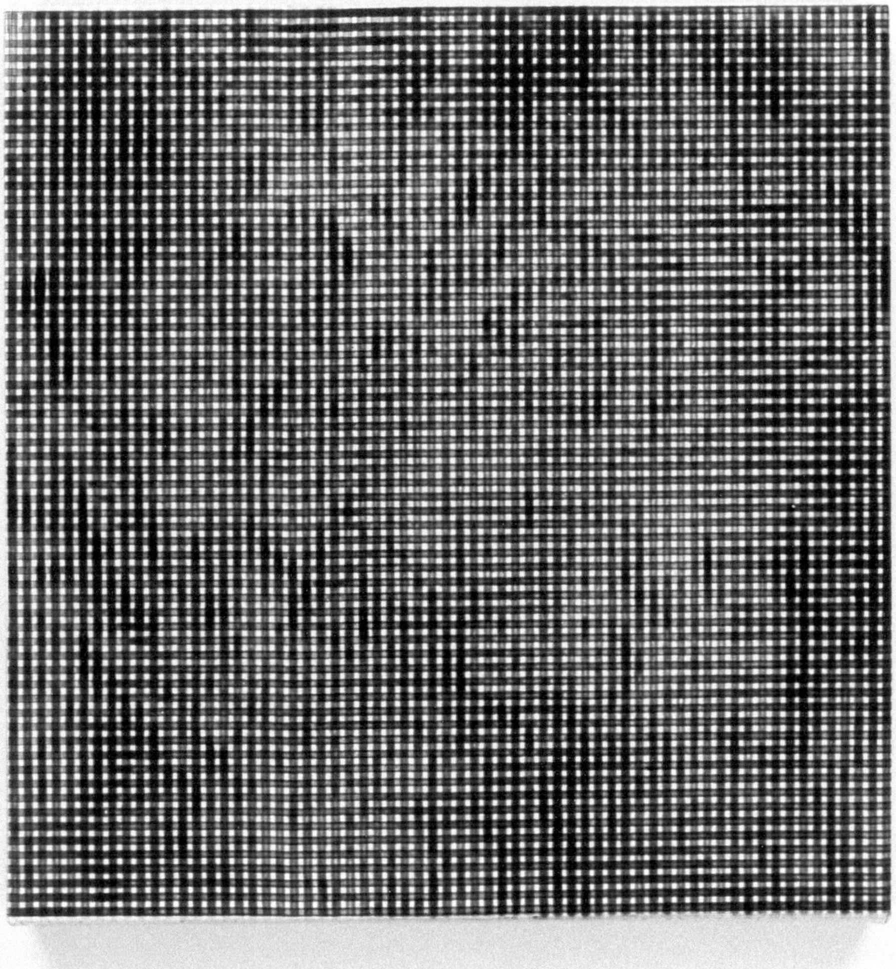

DNA III, 1979

Untitled II, 1979

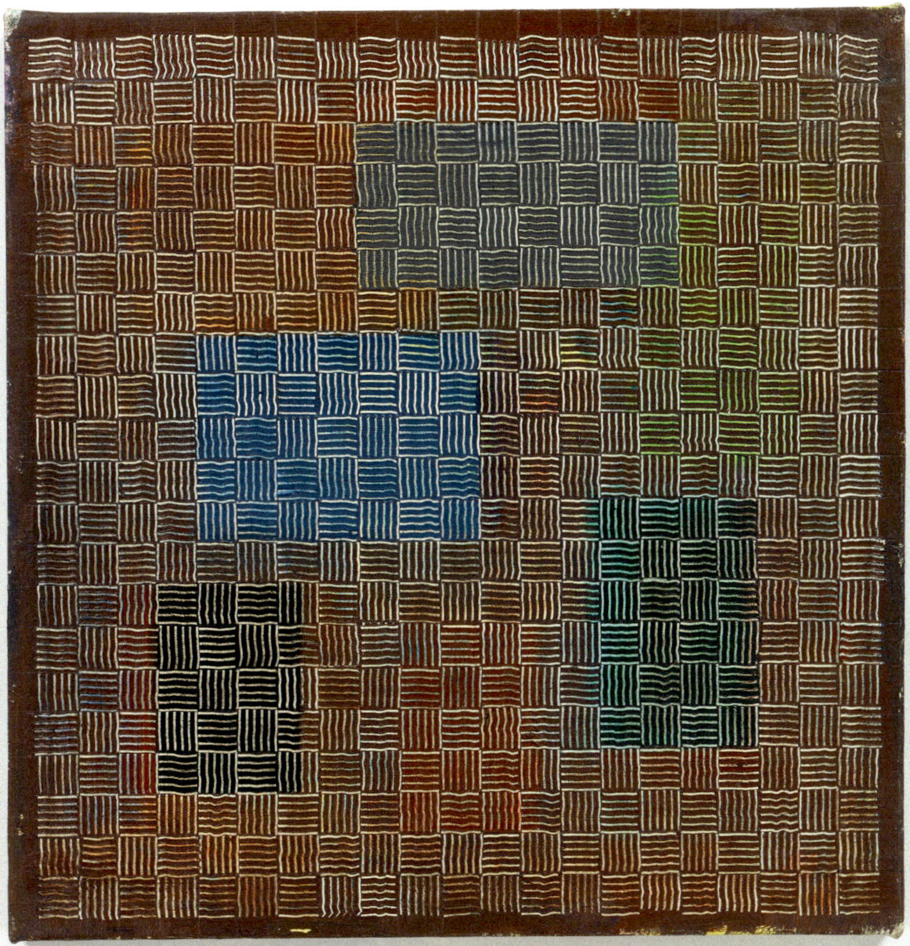

Confirmation I: Happy Birthday Mary, 1979

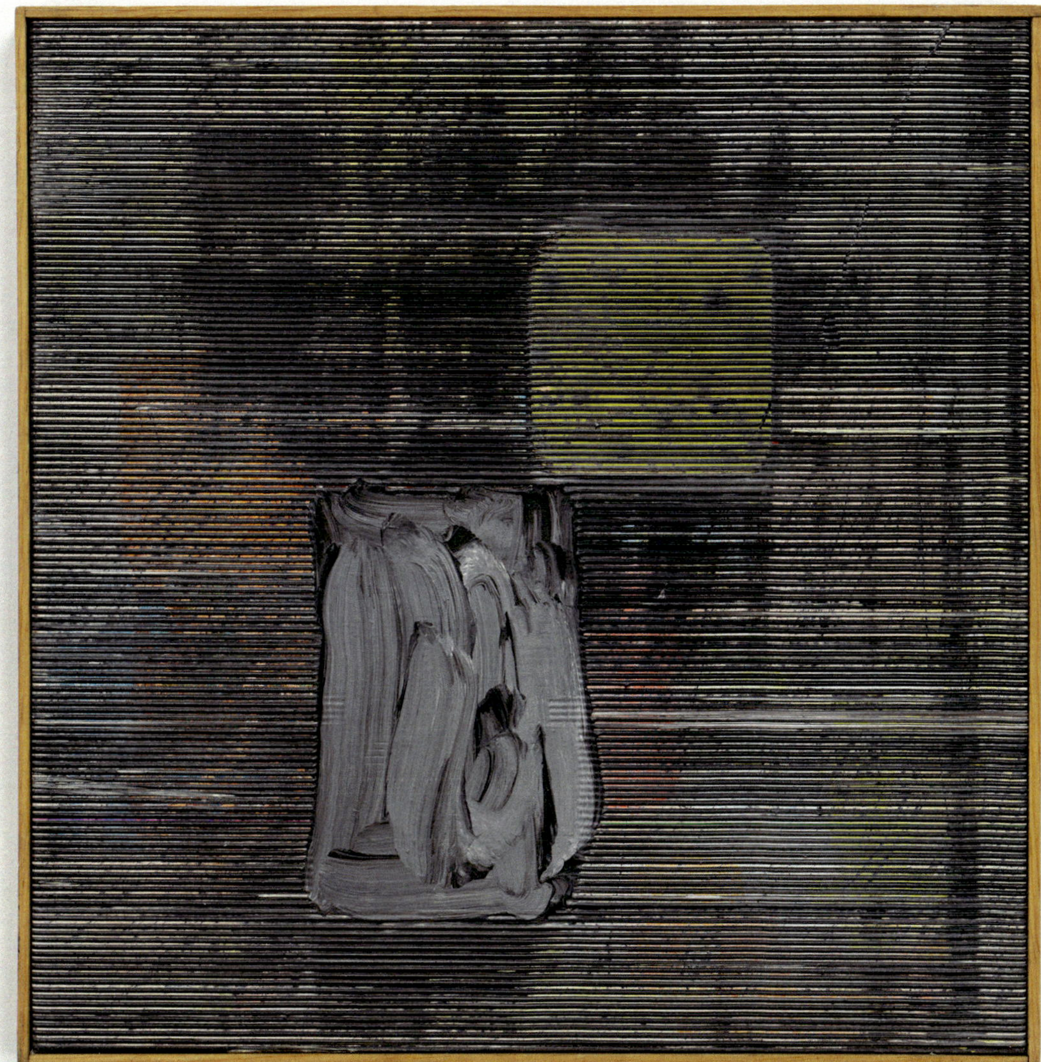

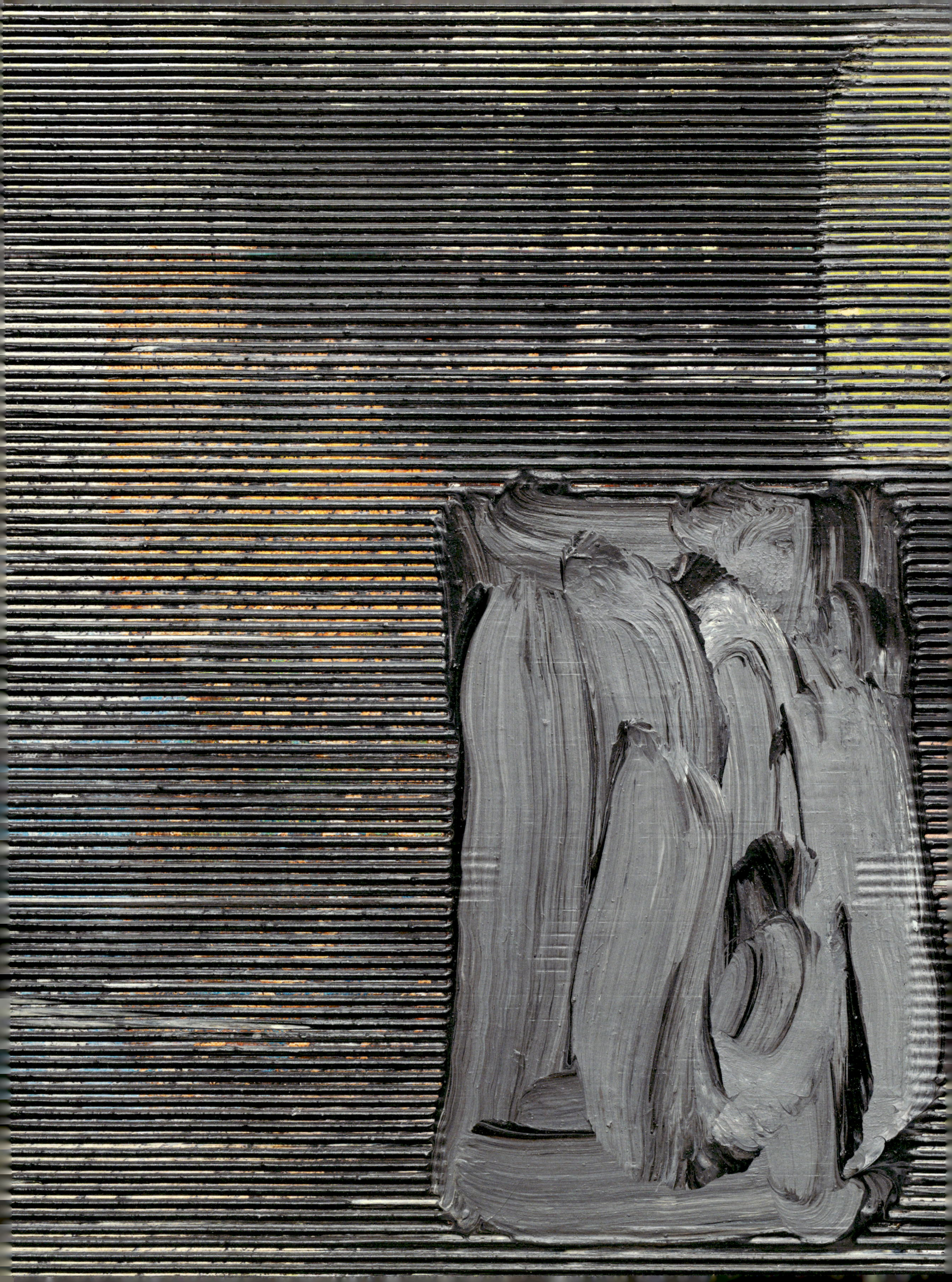

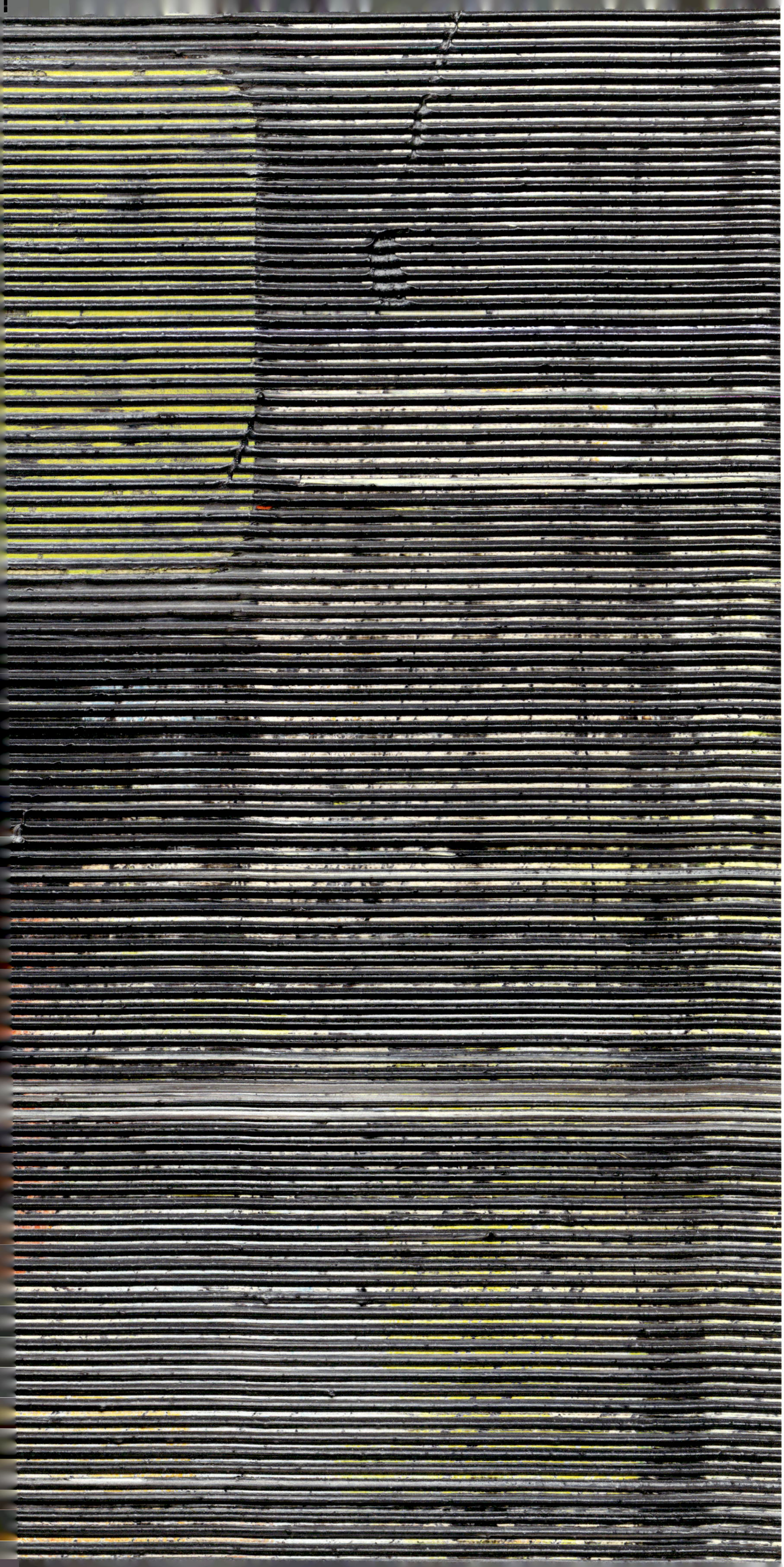

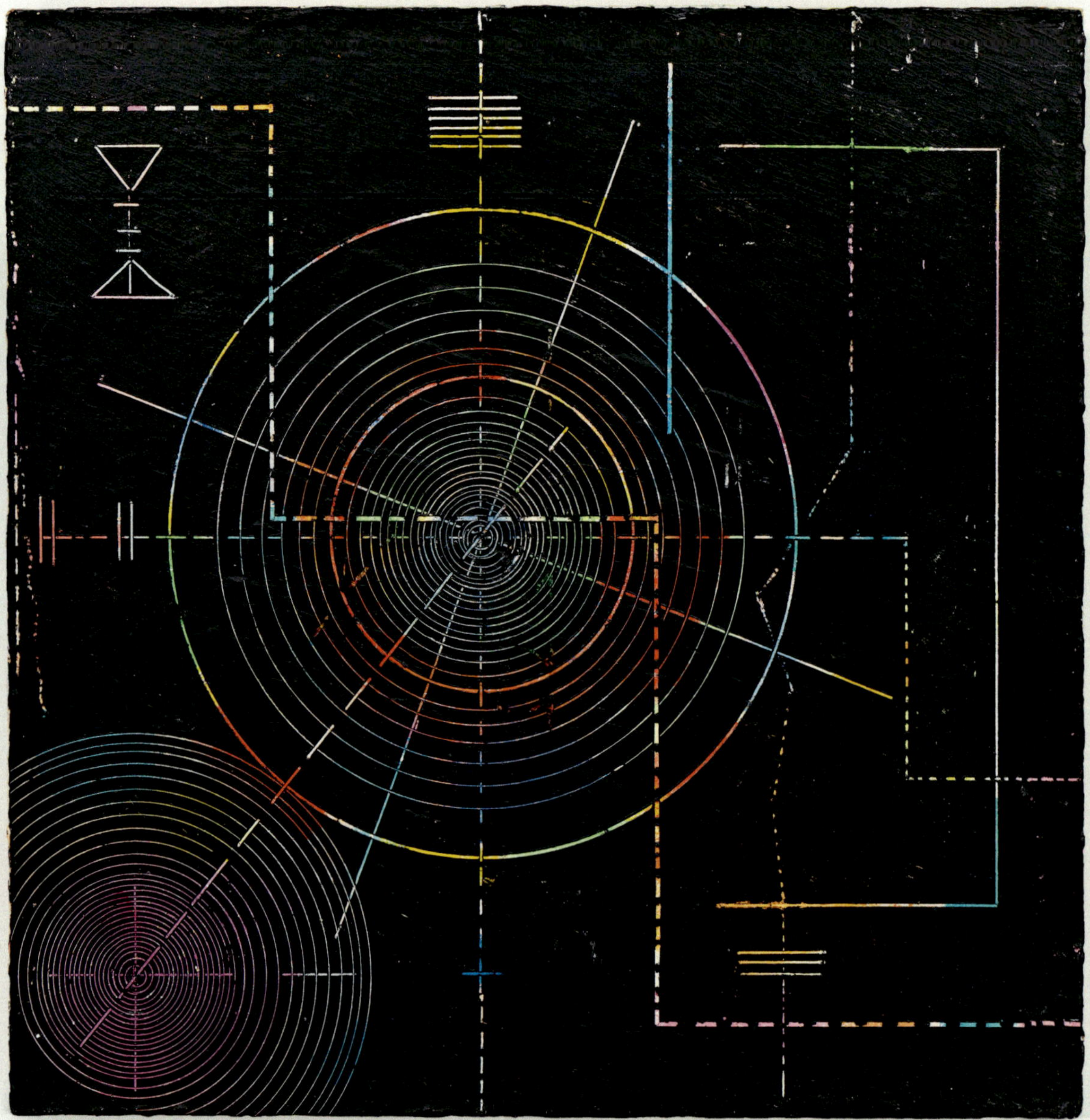

Black in Time I, 1980

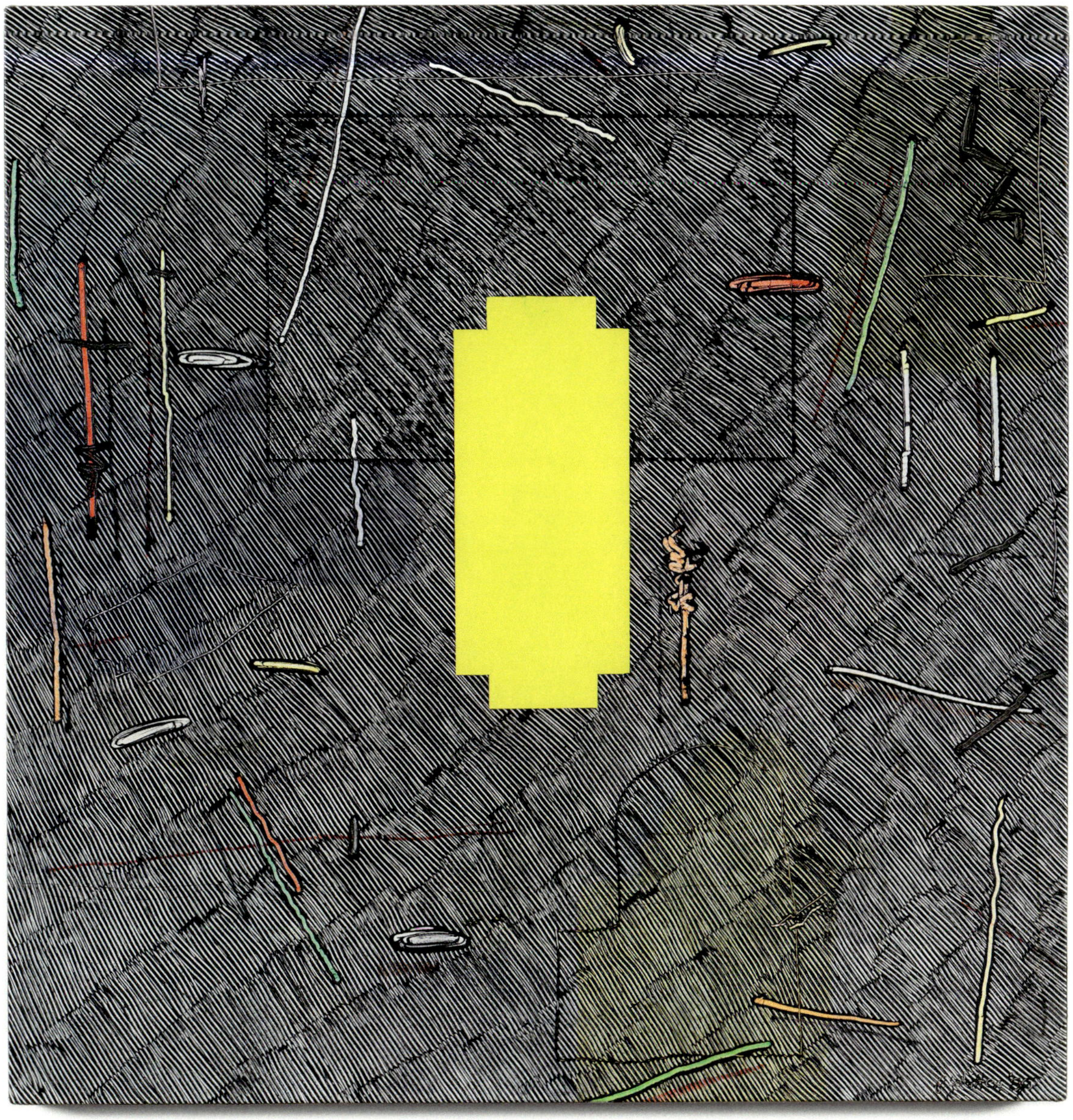

Yellow Cross for Naomi, 1980

Annabelle II, 1984

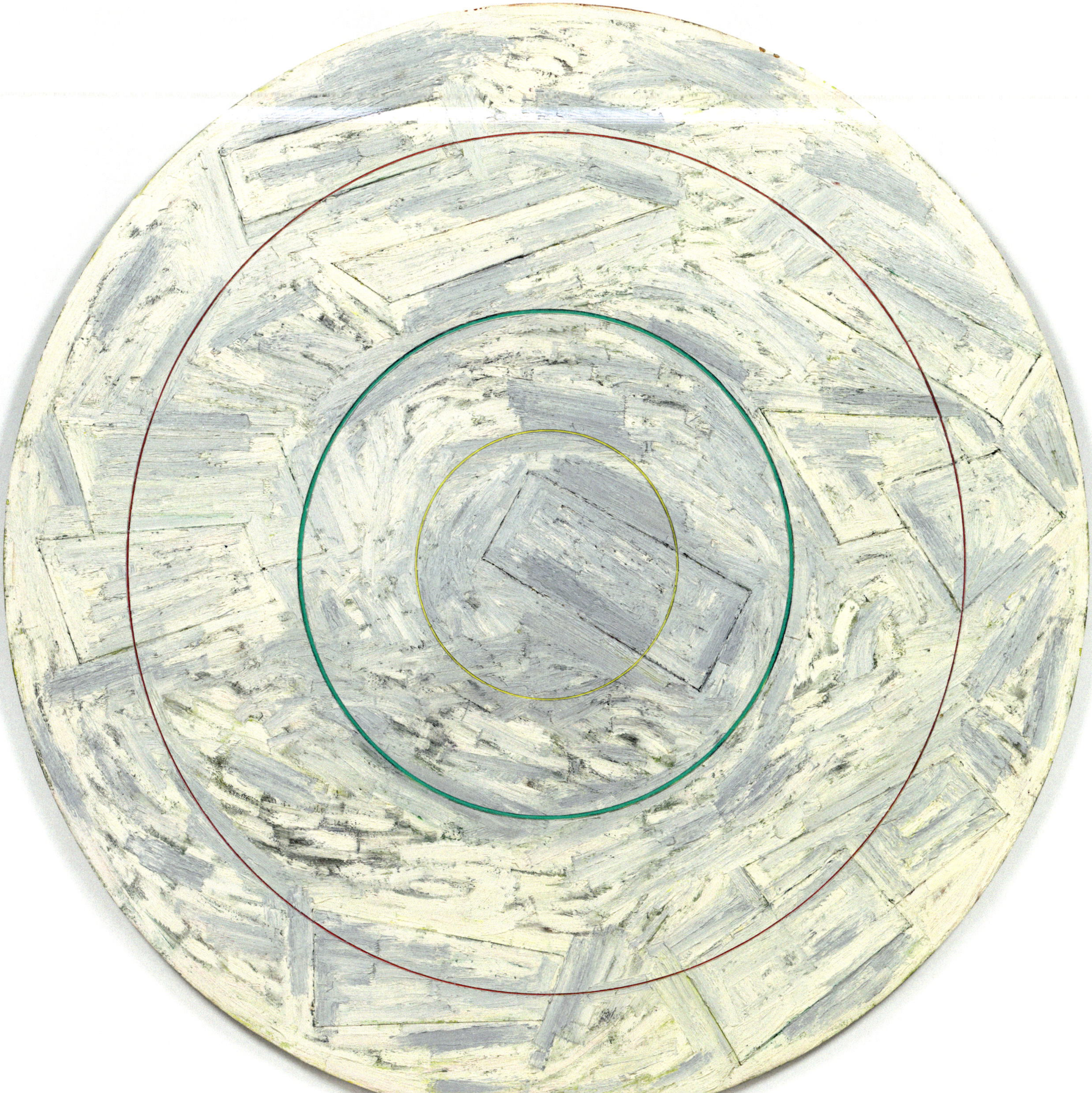

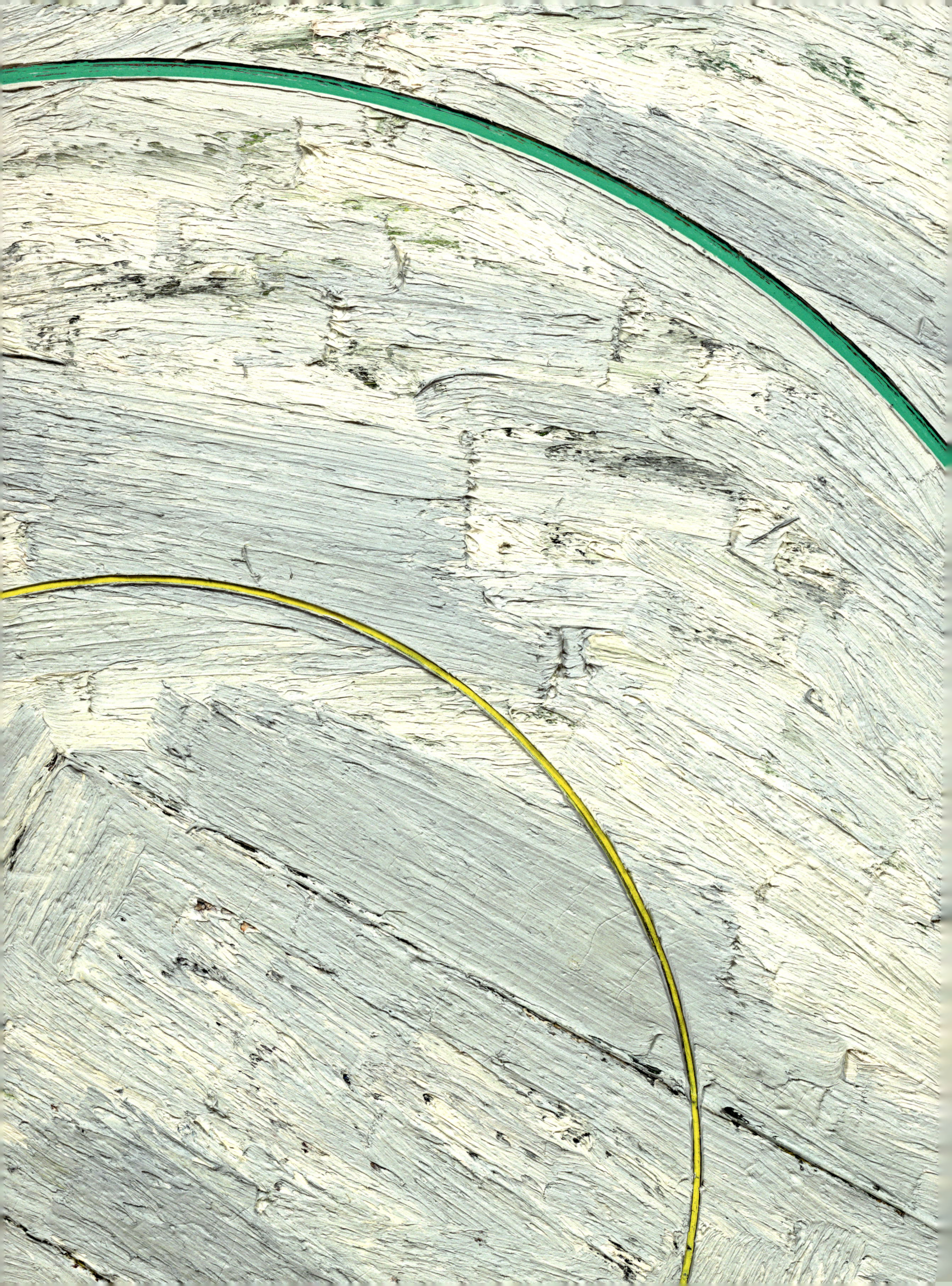

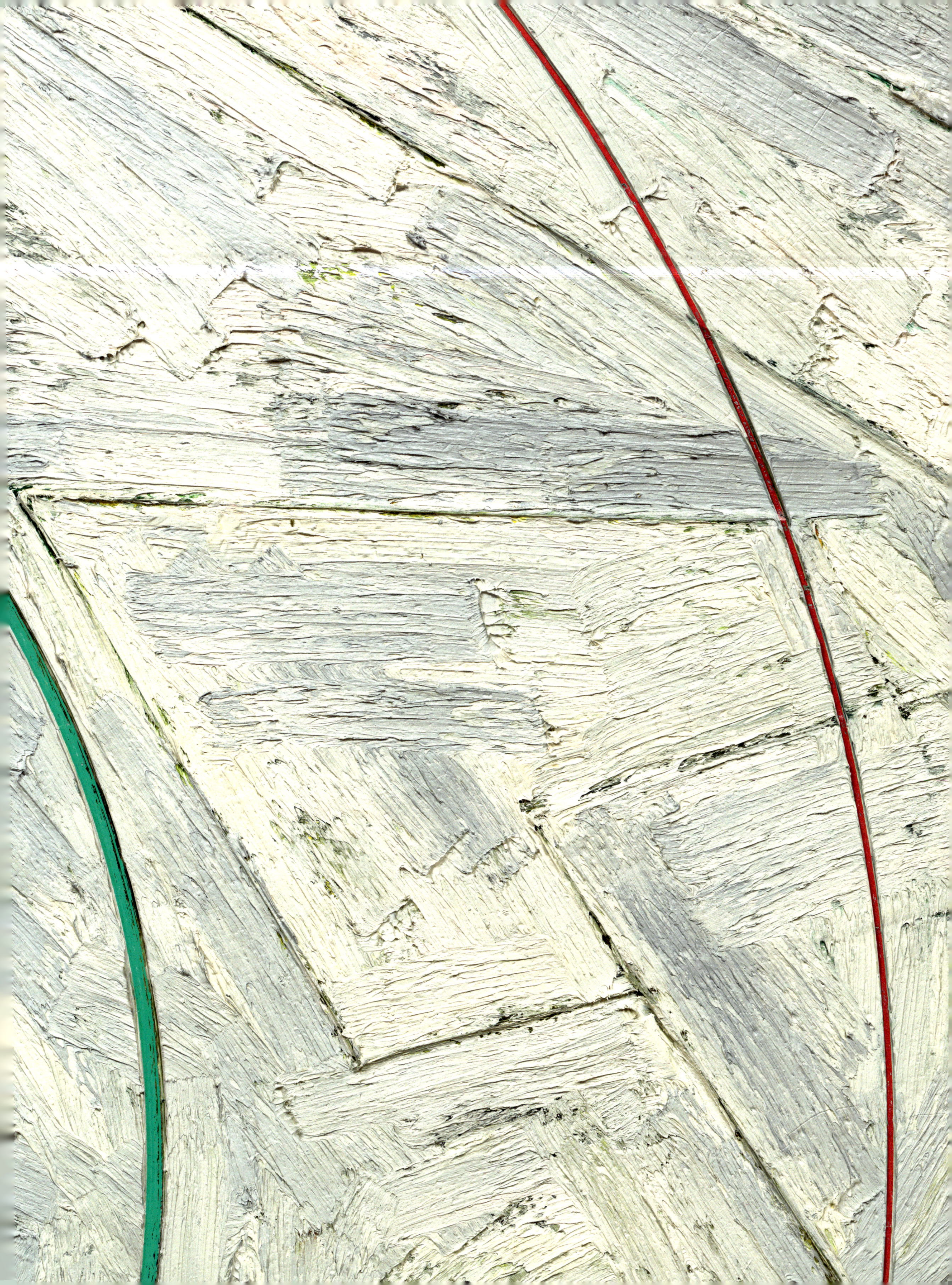

To My Valentine, 1984

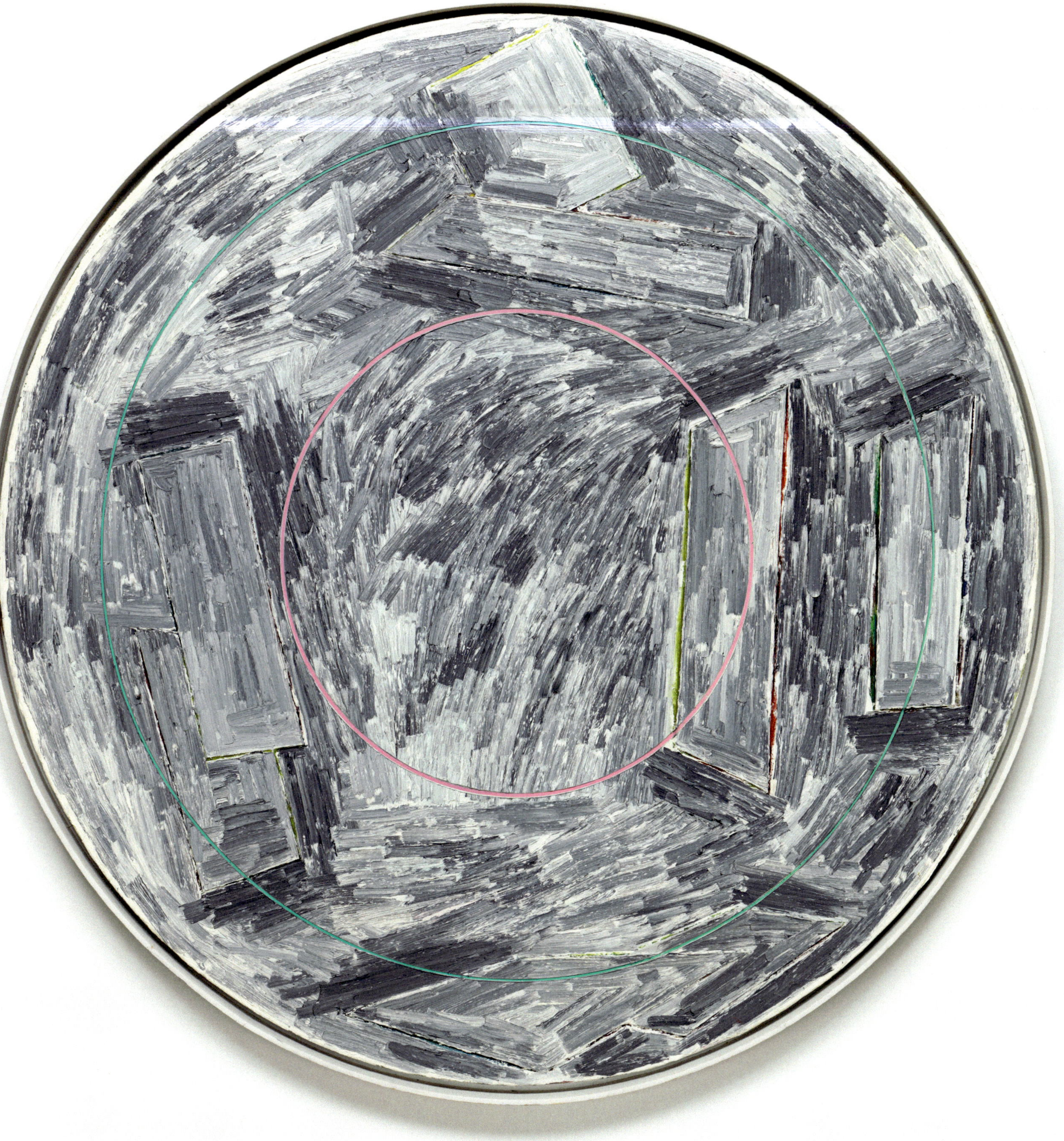

Soweto Disk II AKA Big O for Obama, 1985

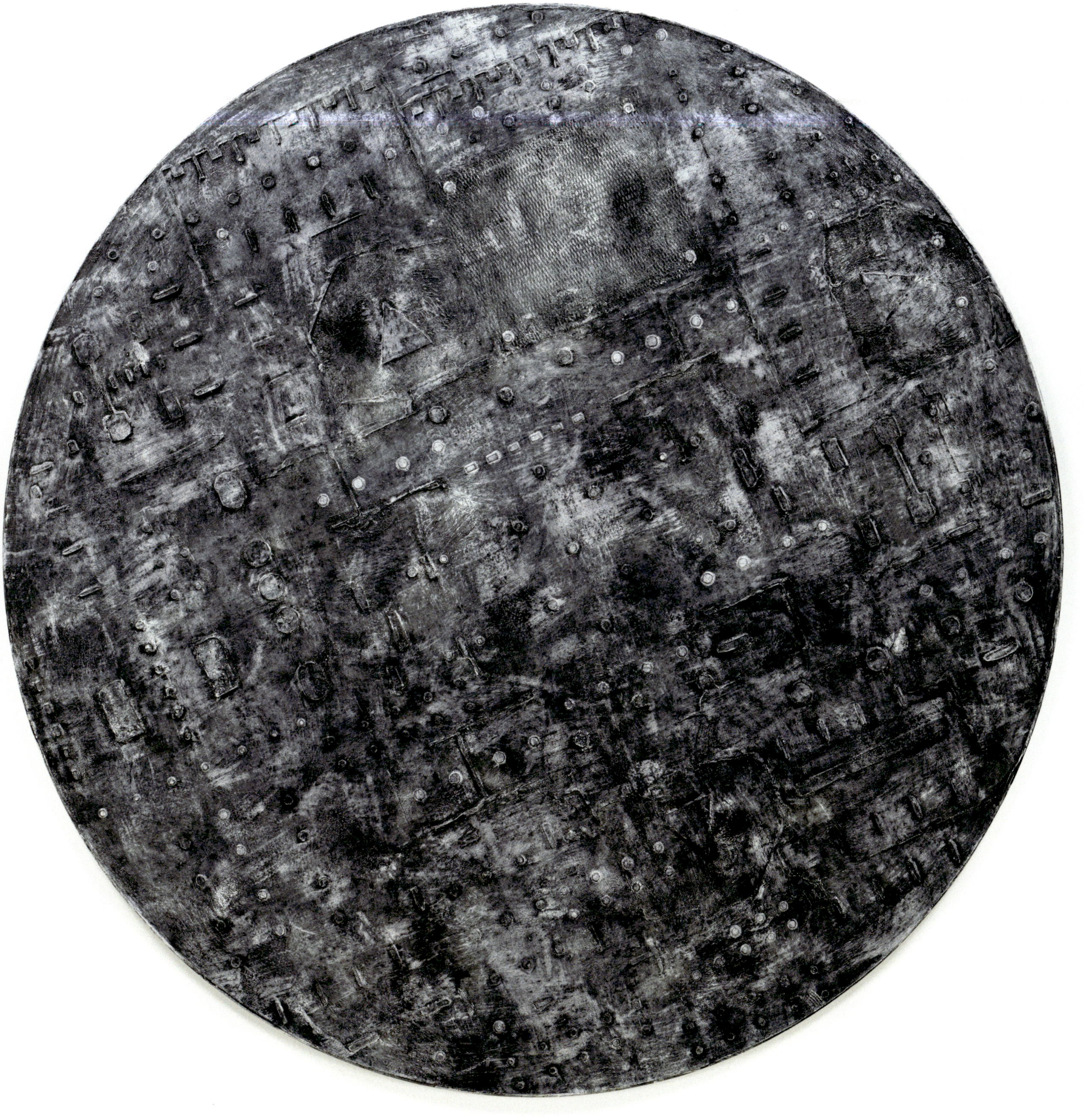

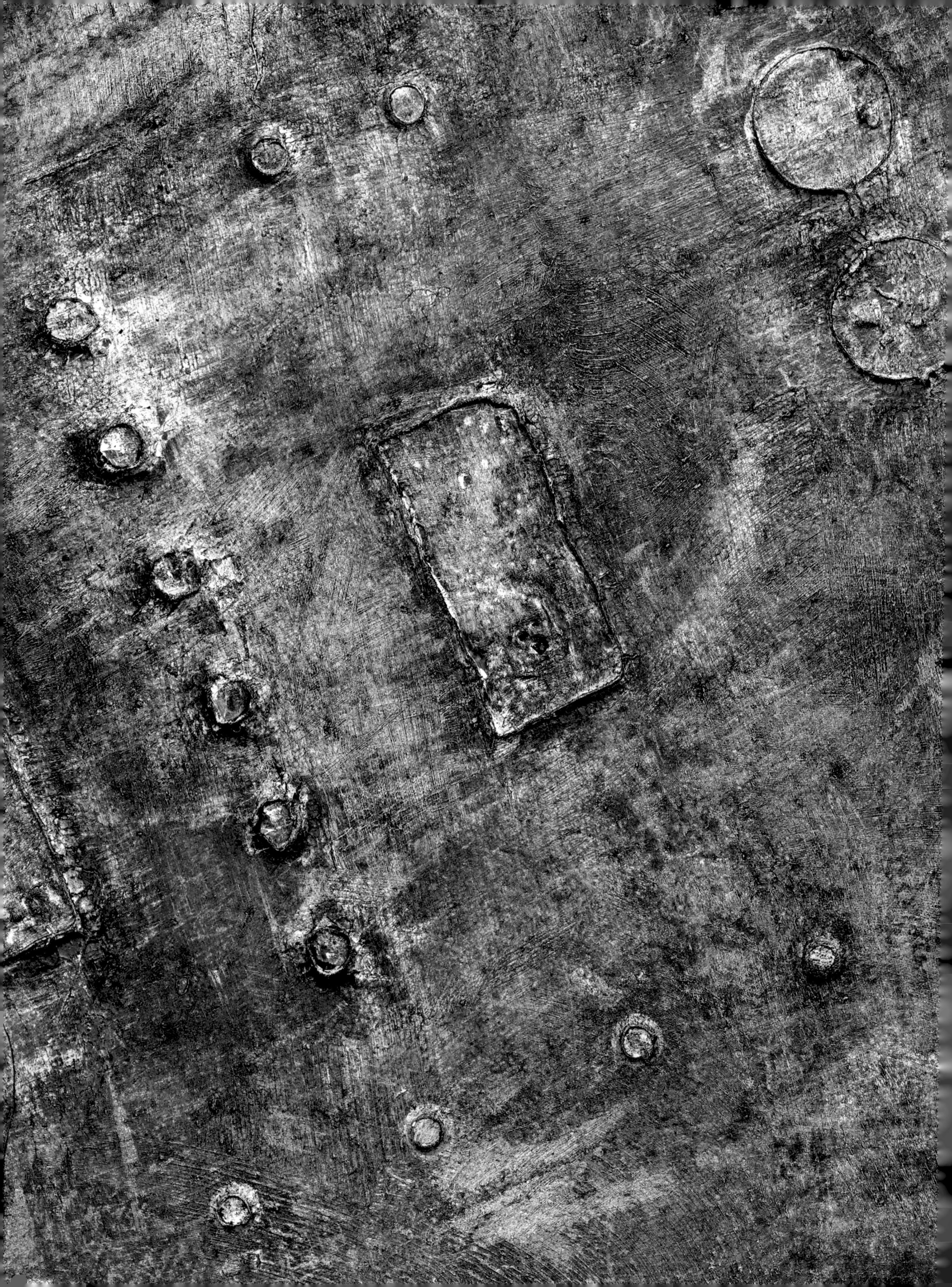

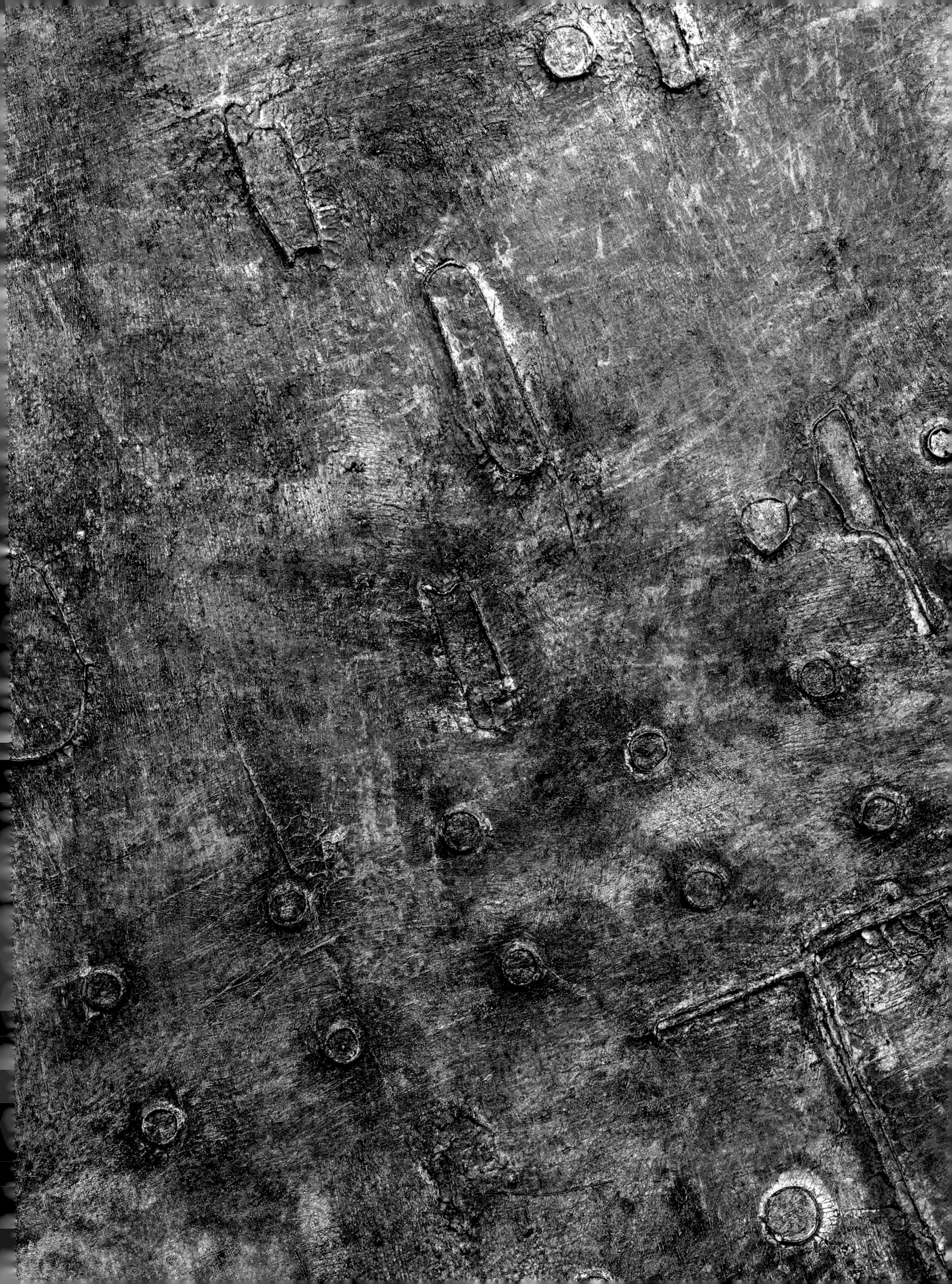

The Kid from Red Bank: The Count, 1985

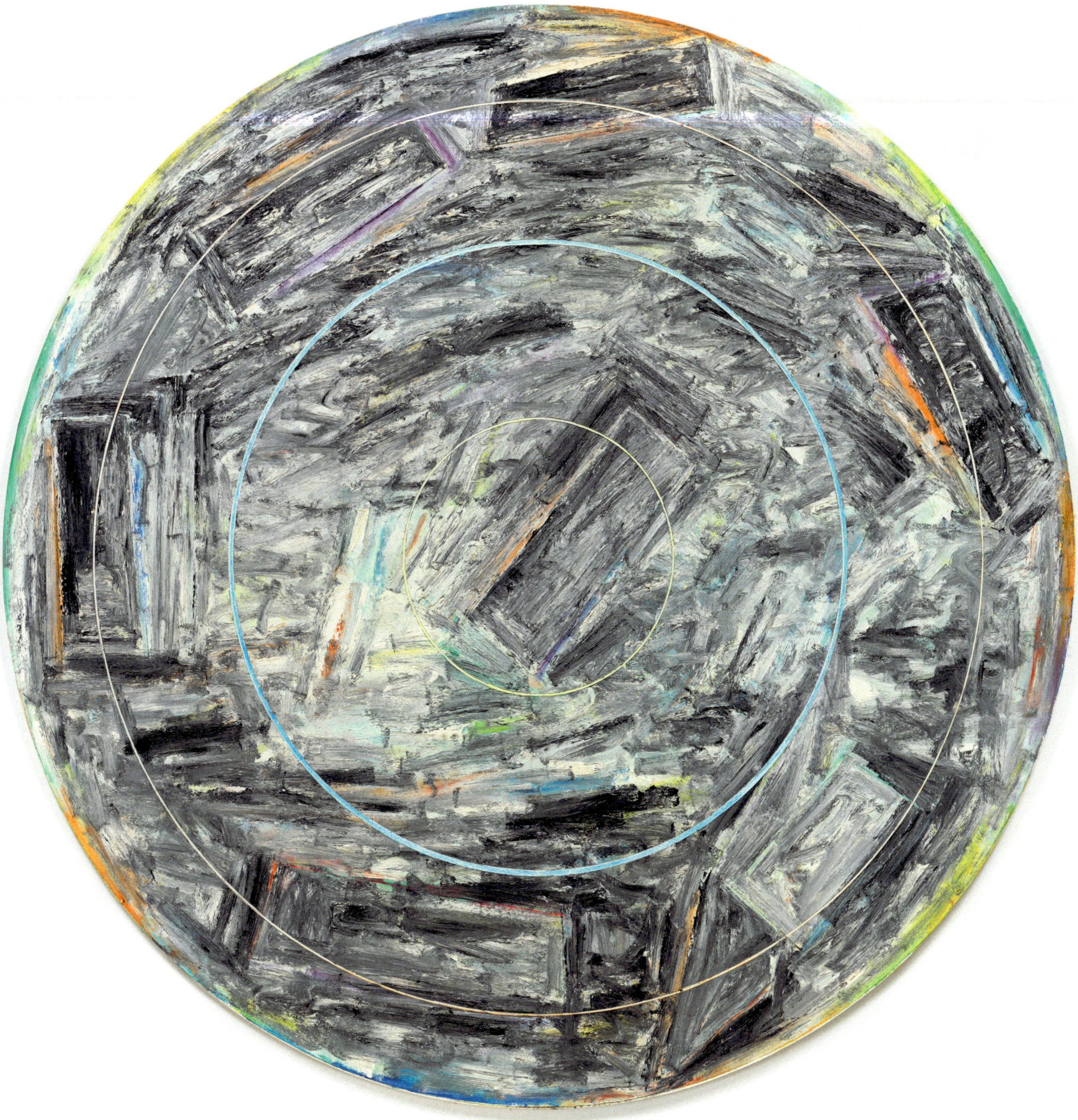

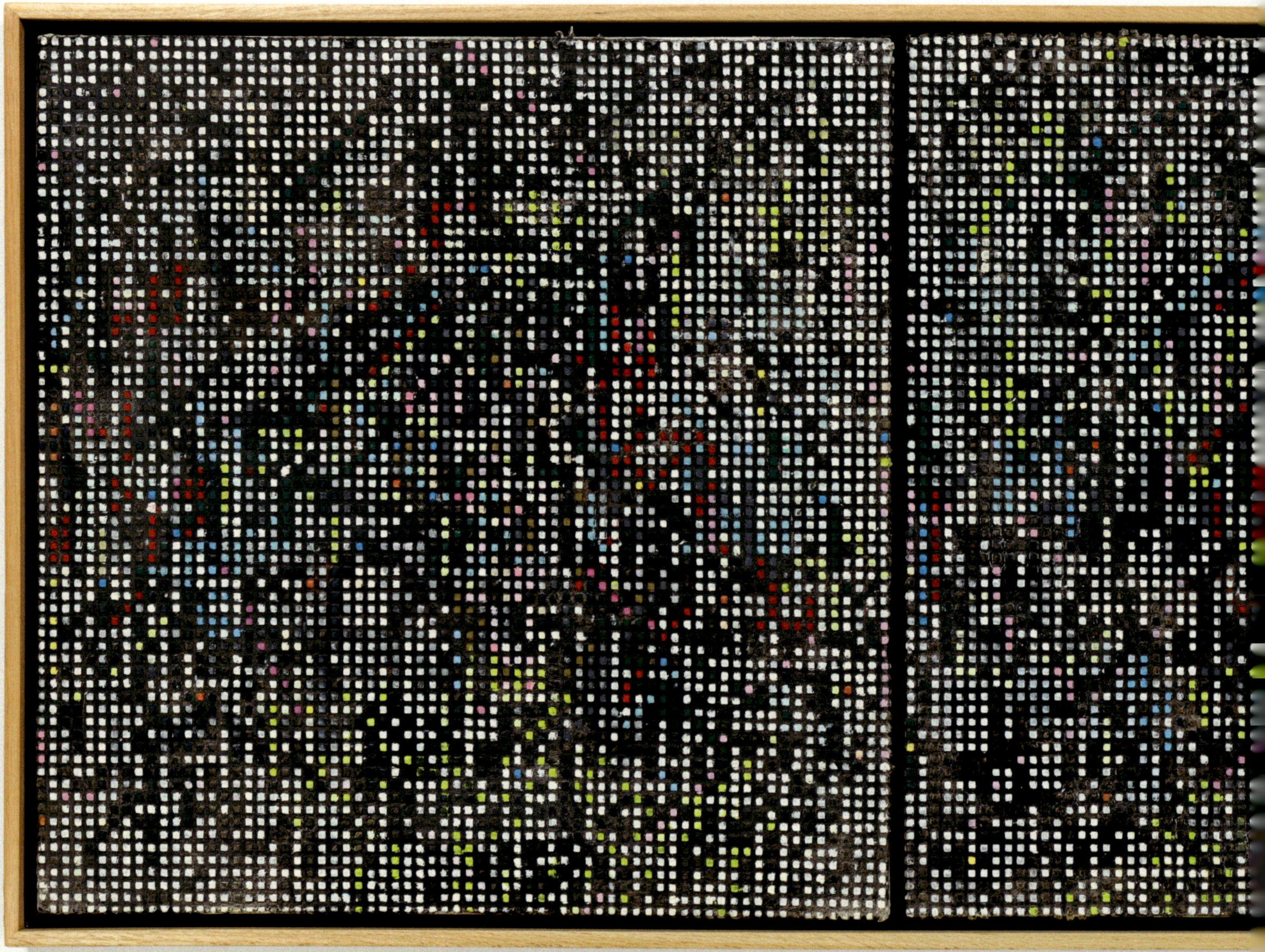

Norman Lewis Triptych I, 1985

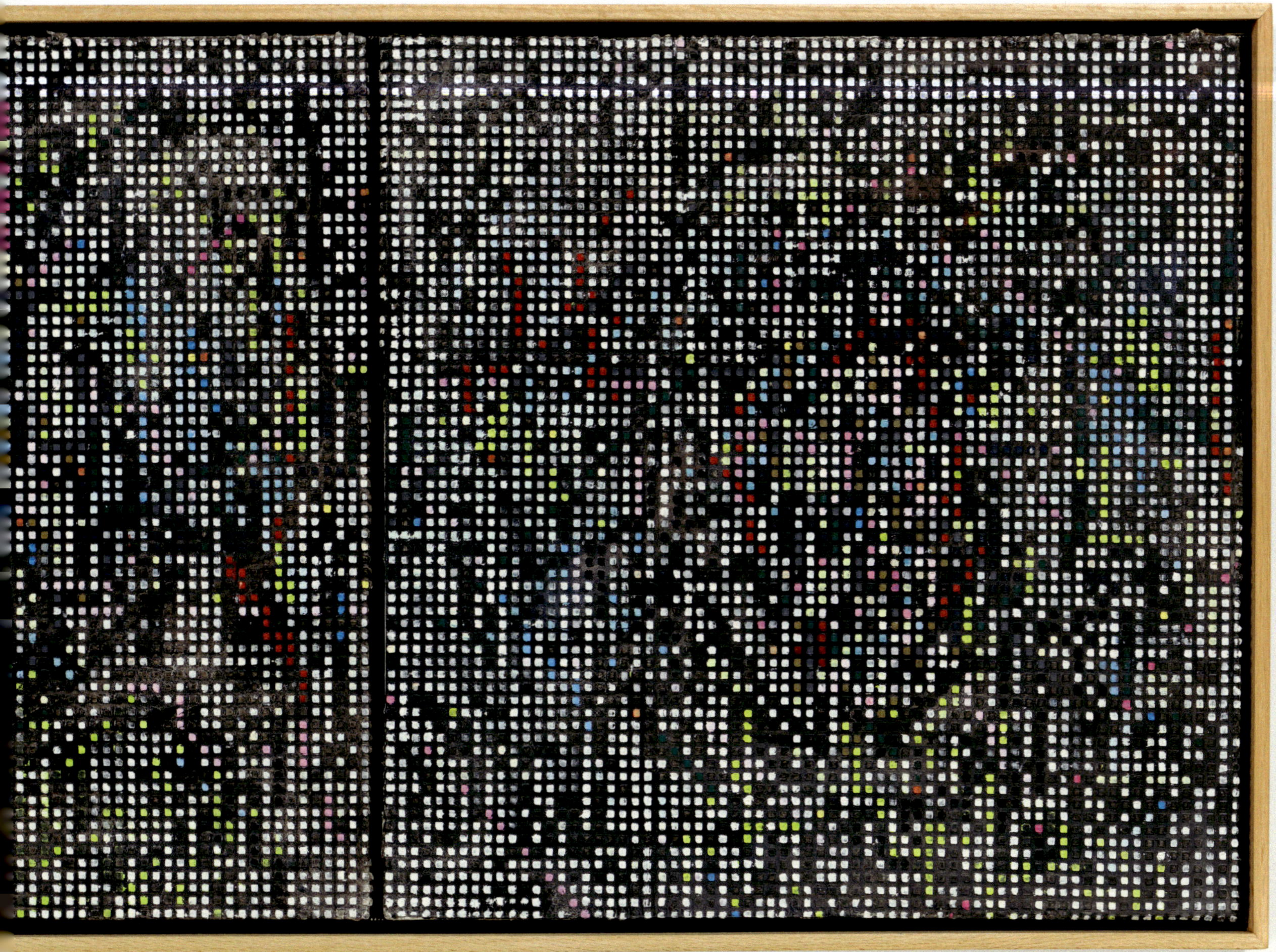

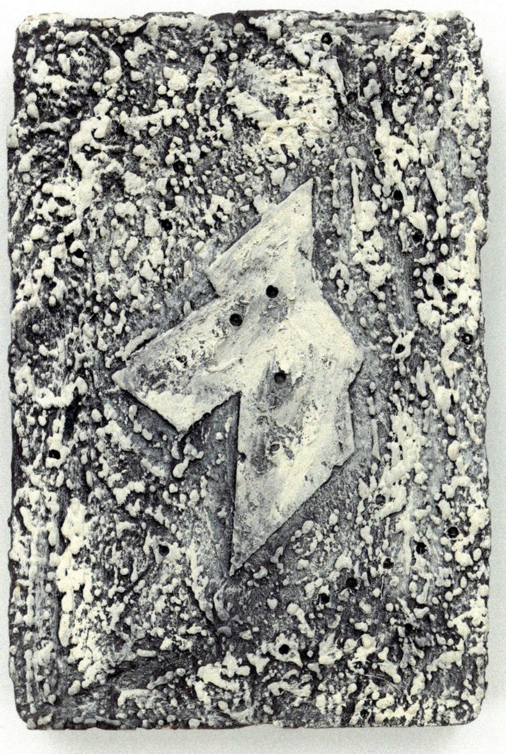

Site I, 1986

Site IV, 1986

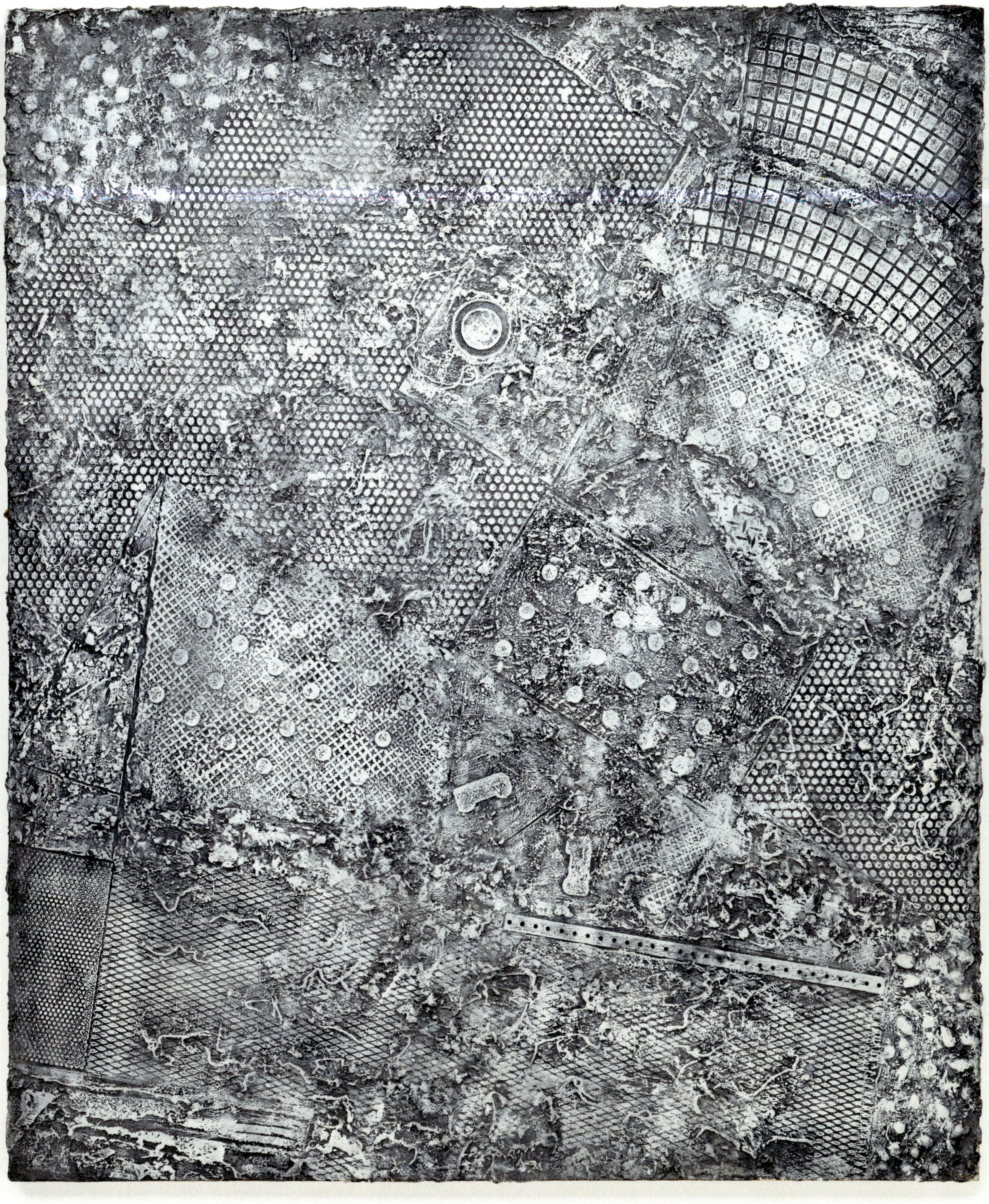

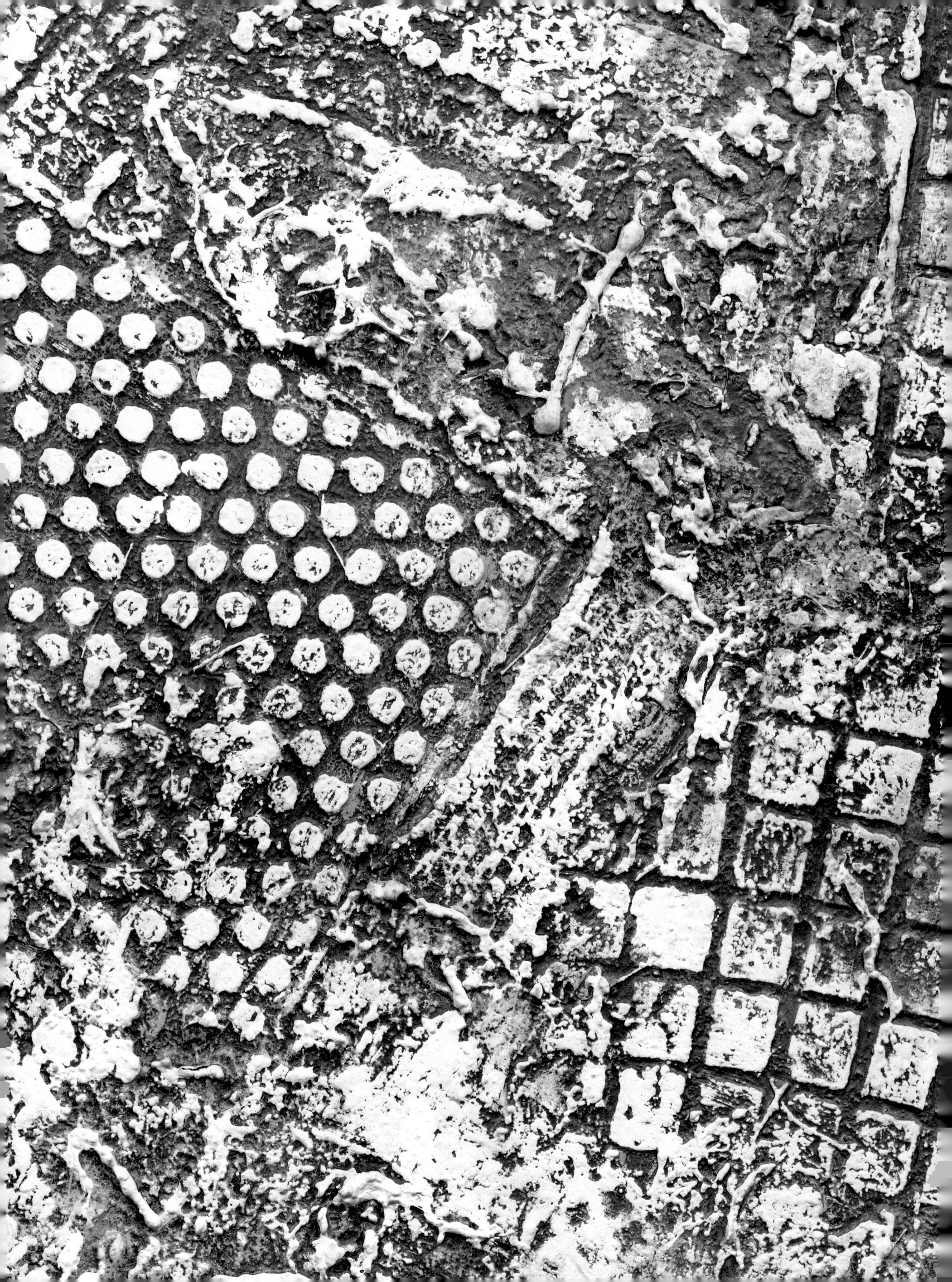

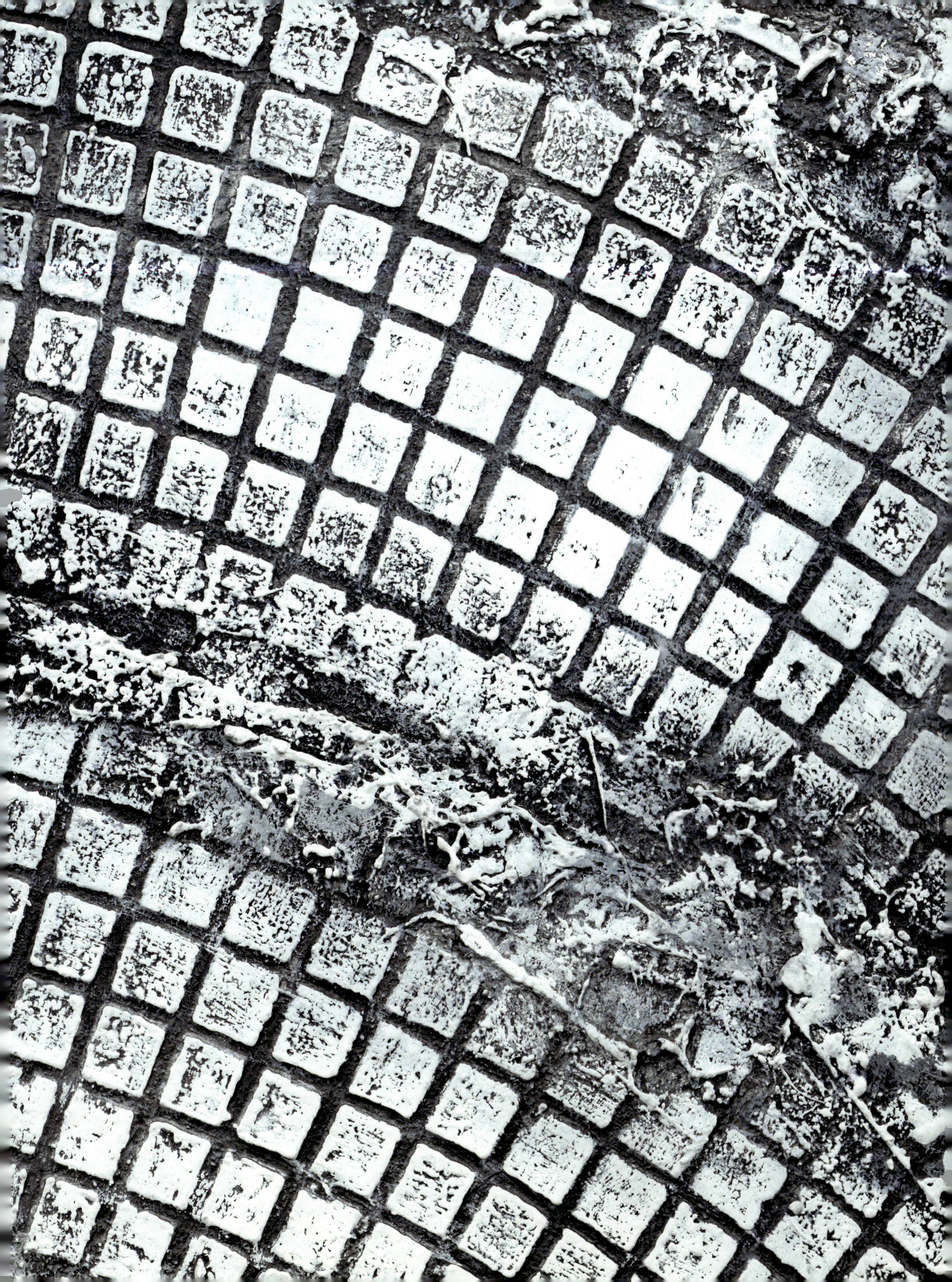

Ode to Andy: For Andy Warhol, 1986

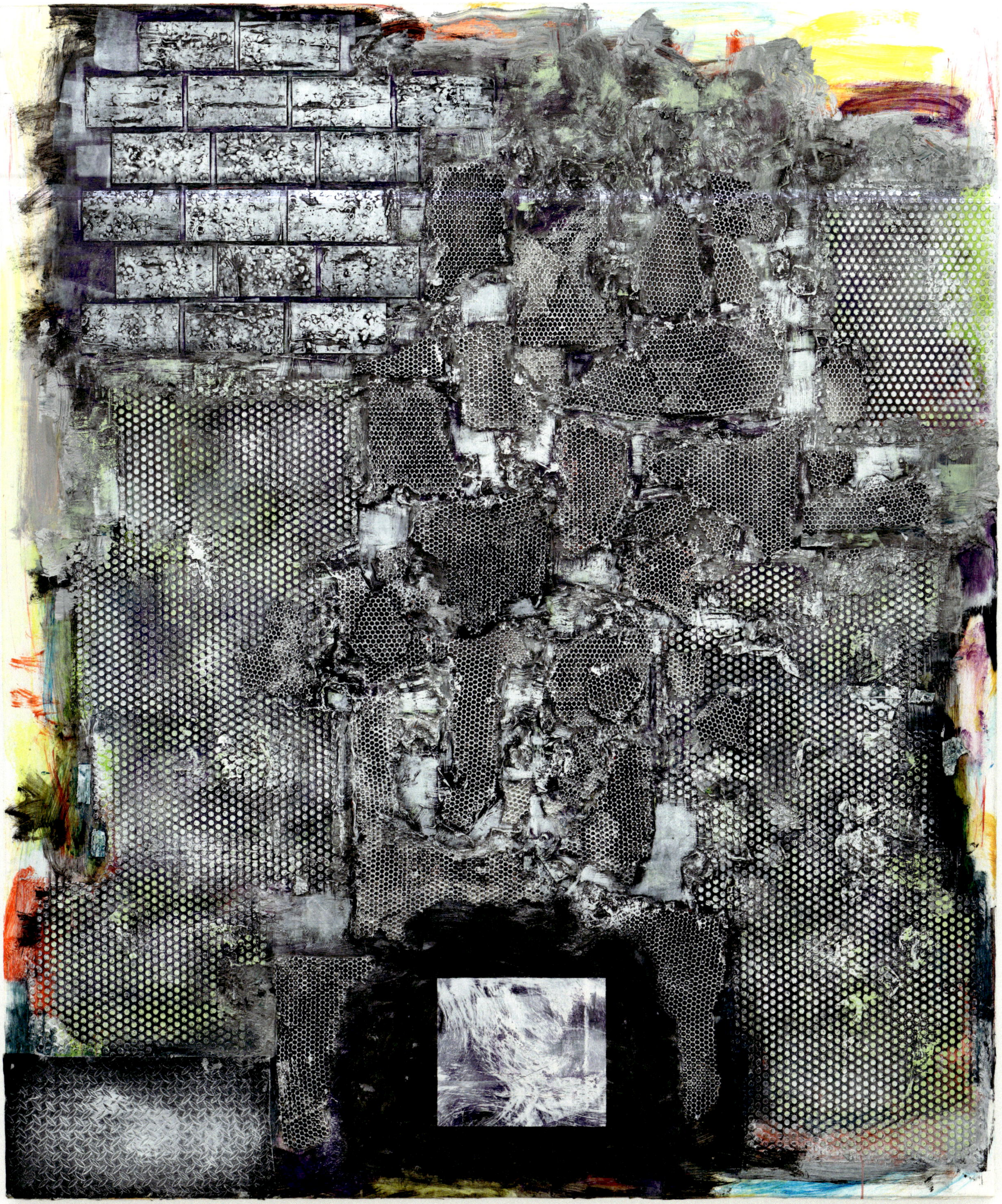

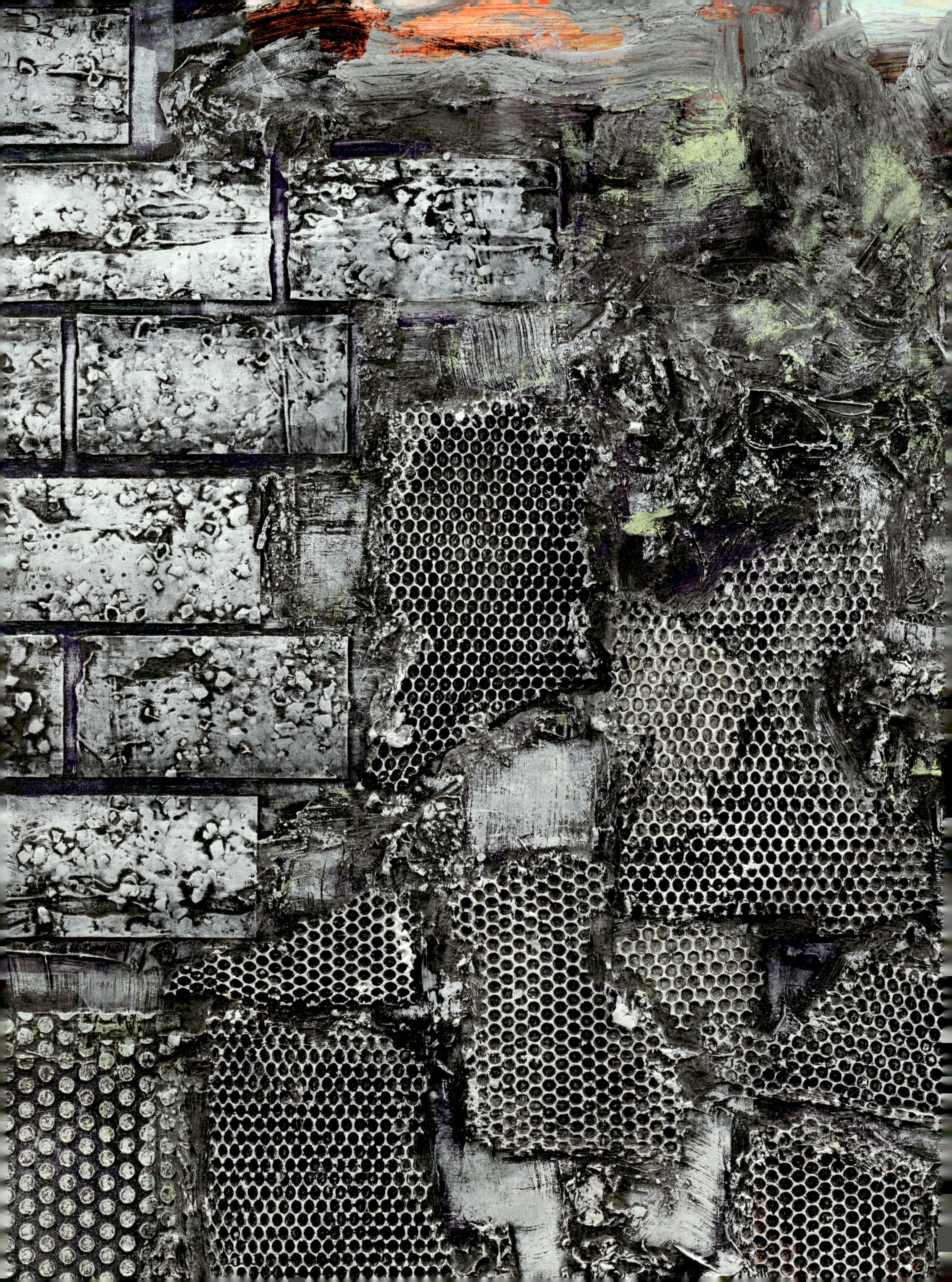

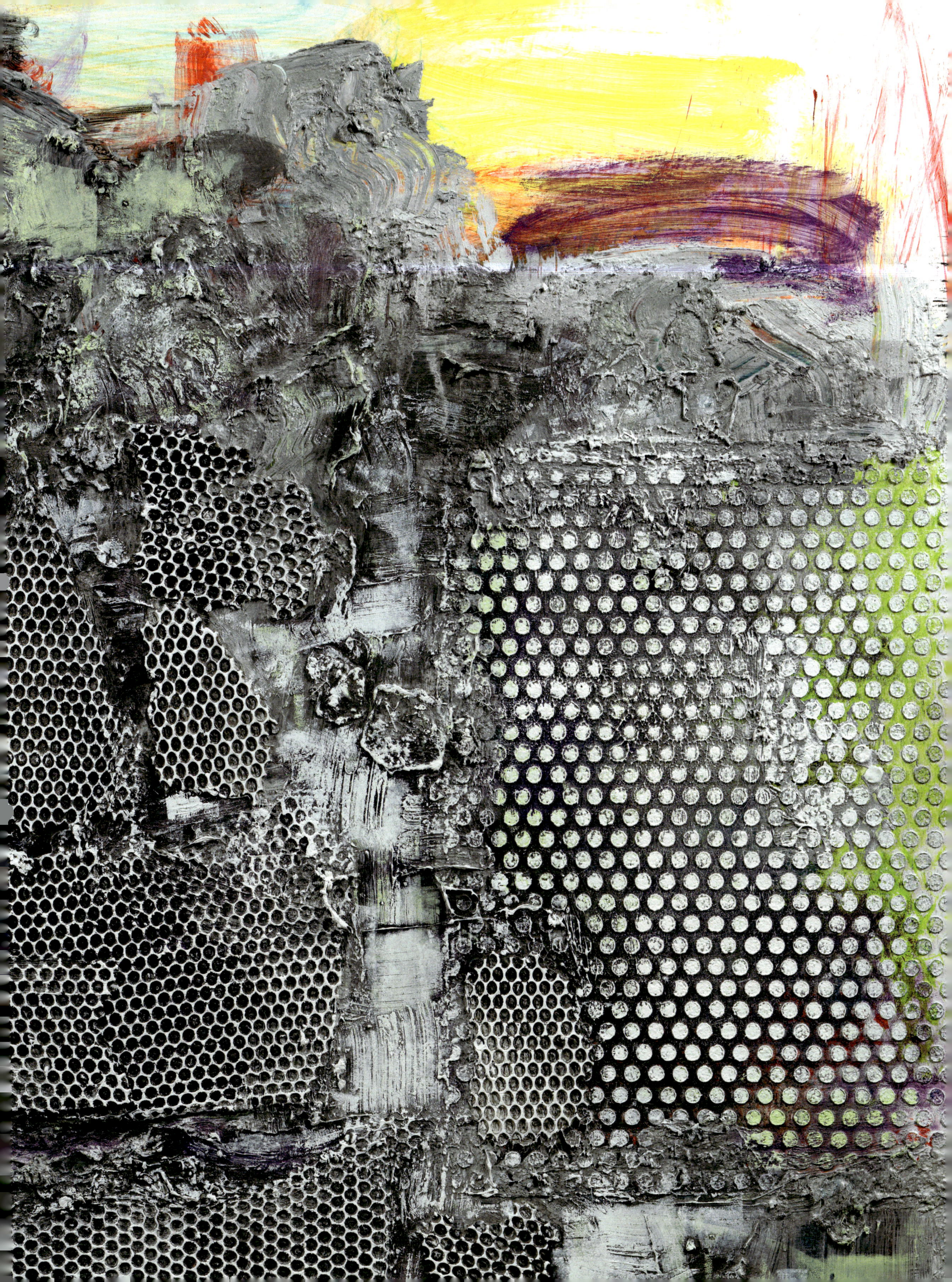

Willi Meets the Keeper (For Willi Smith), 1987

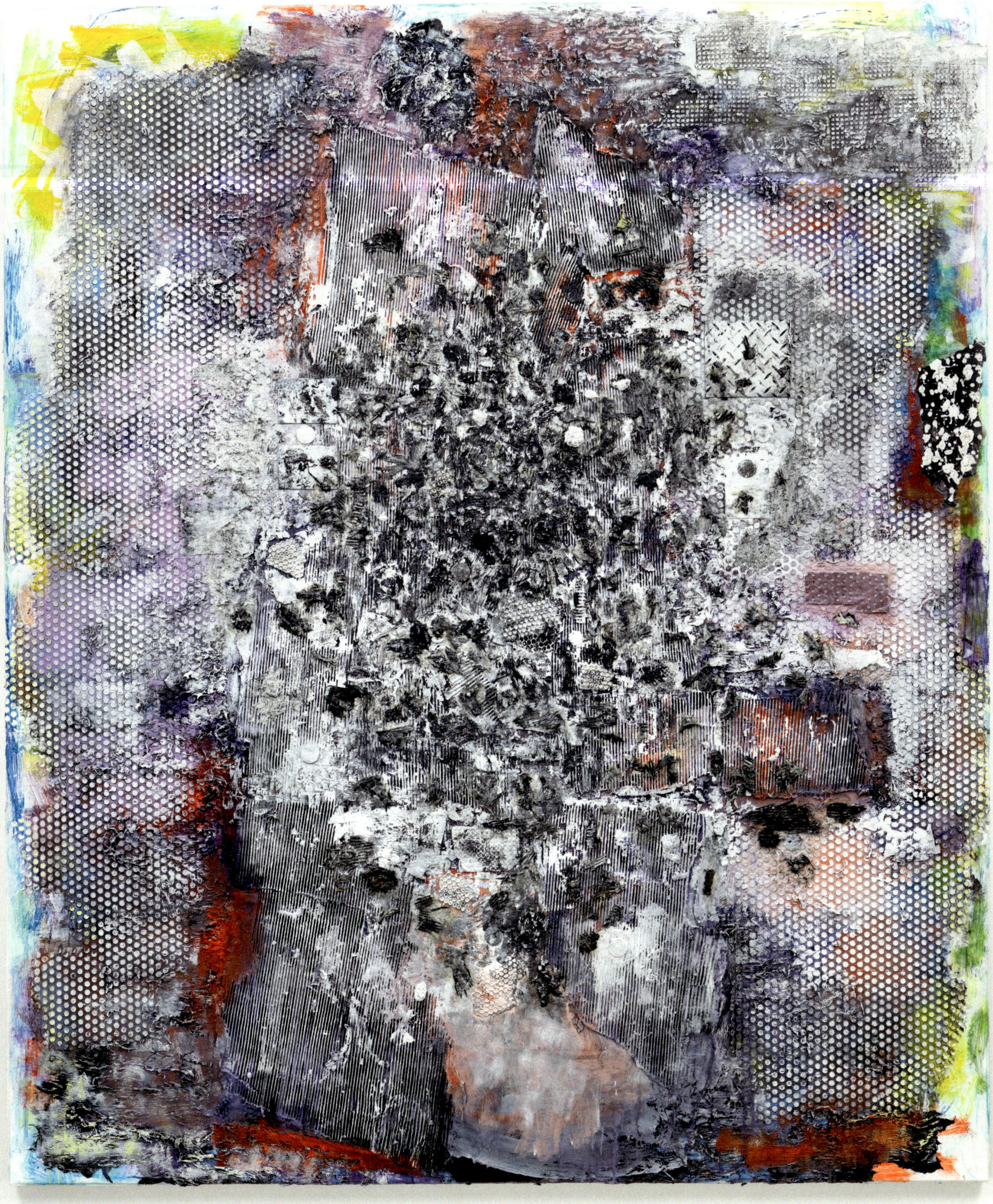

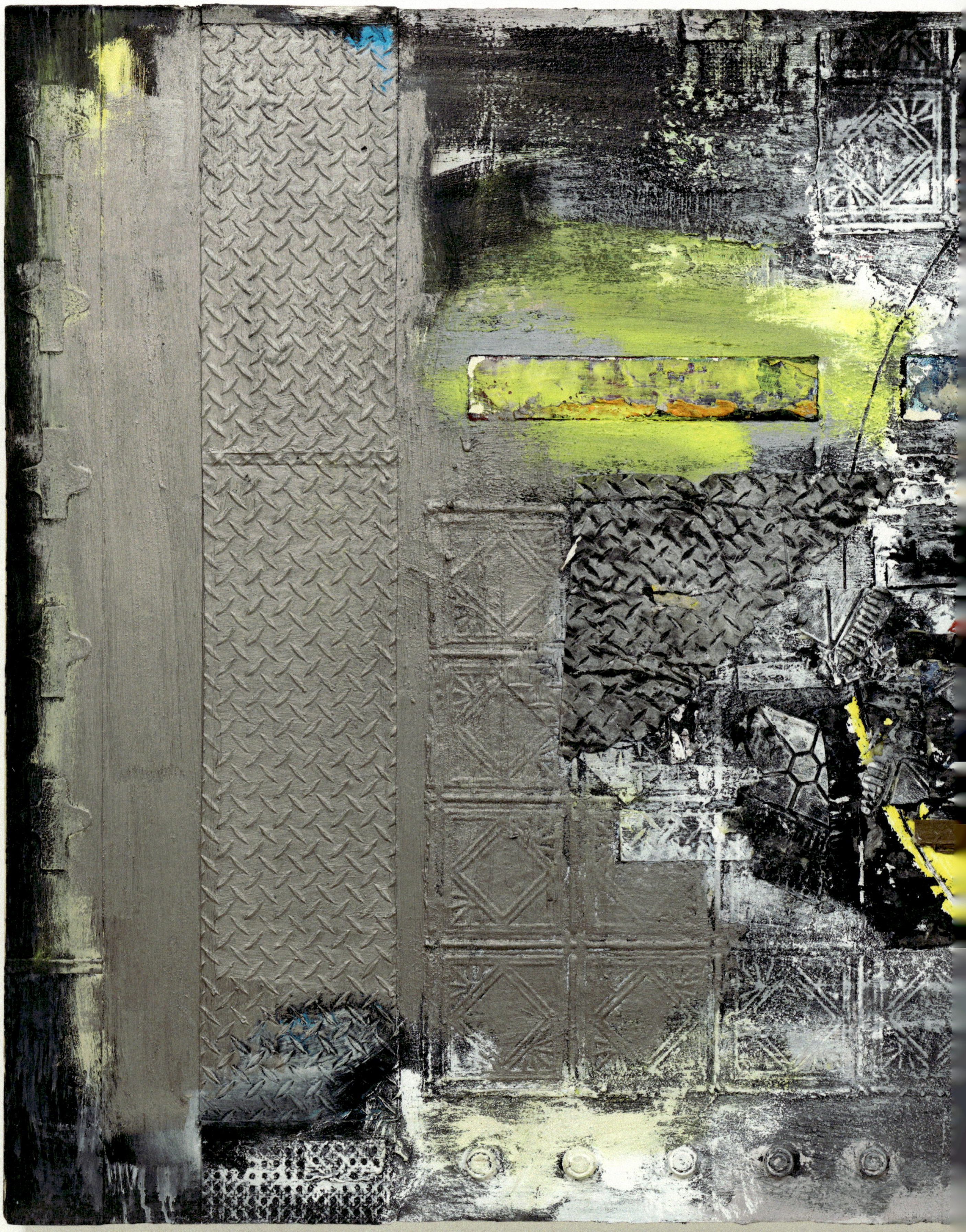

The Alliance, 1988

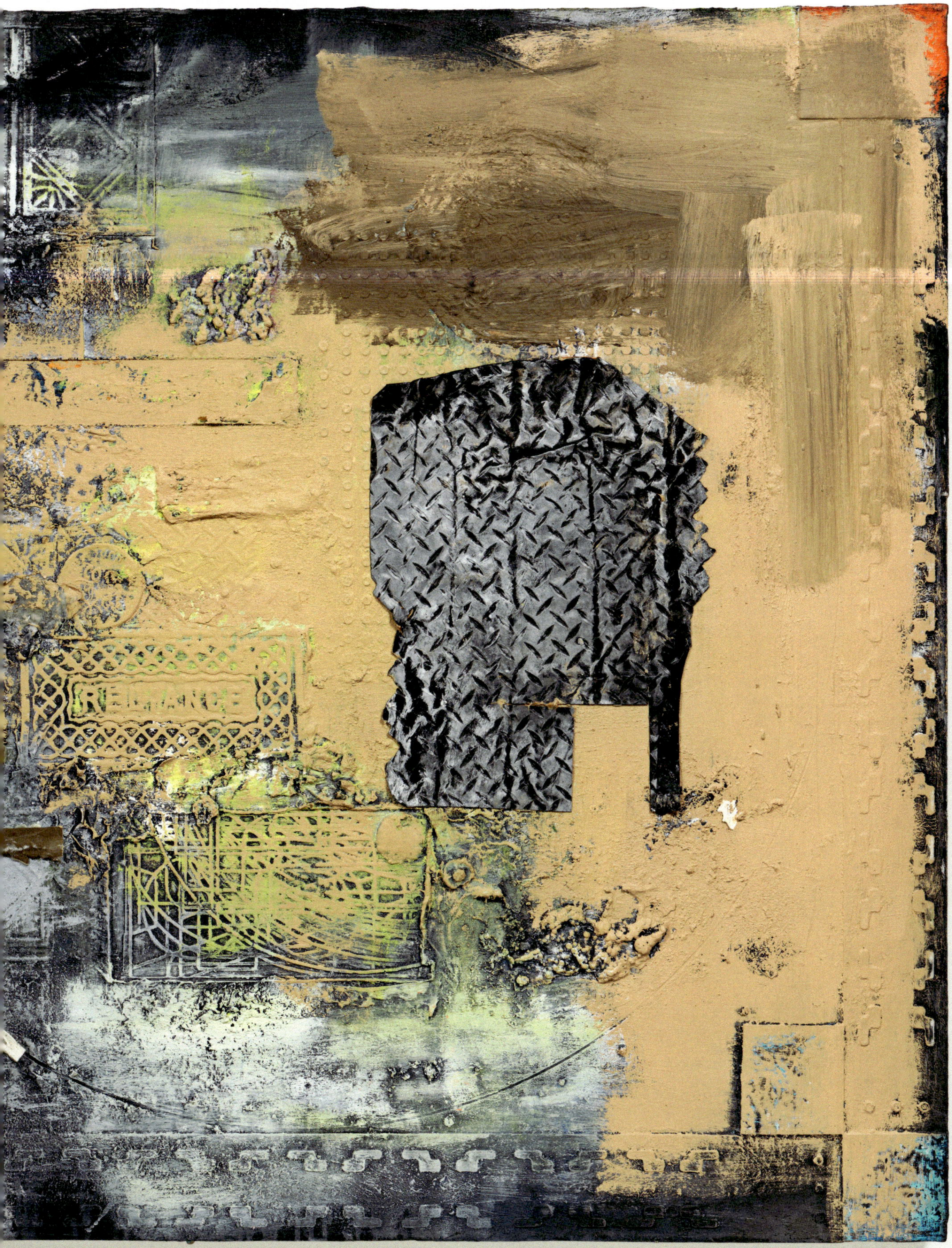

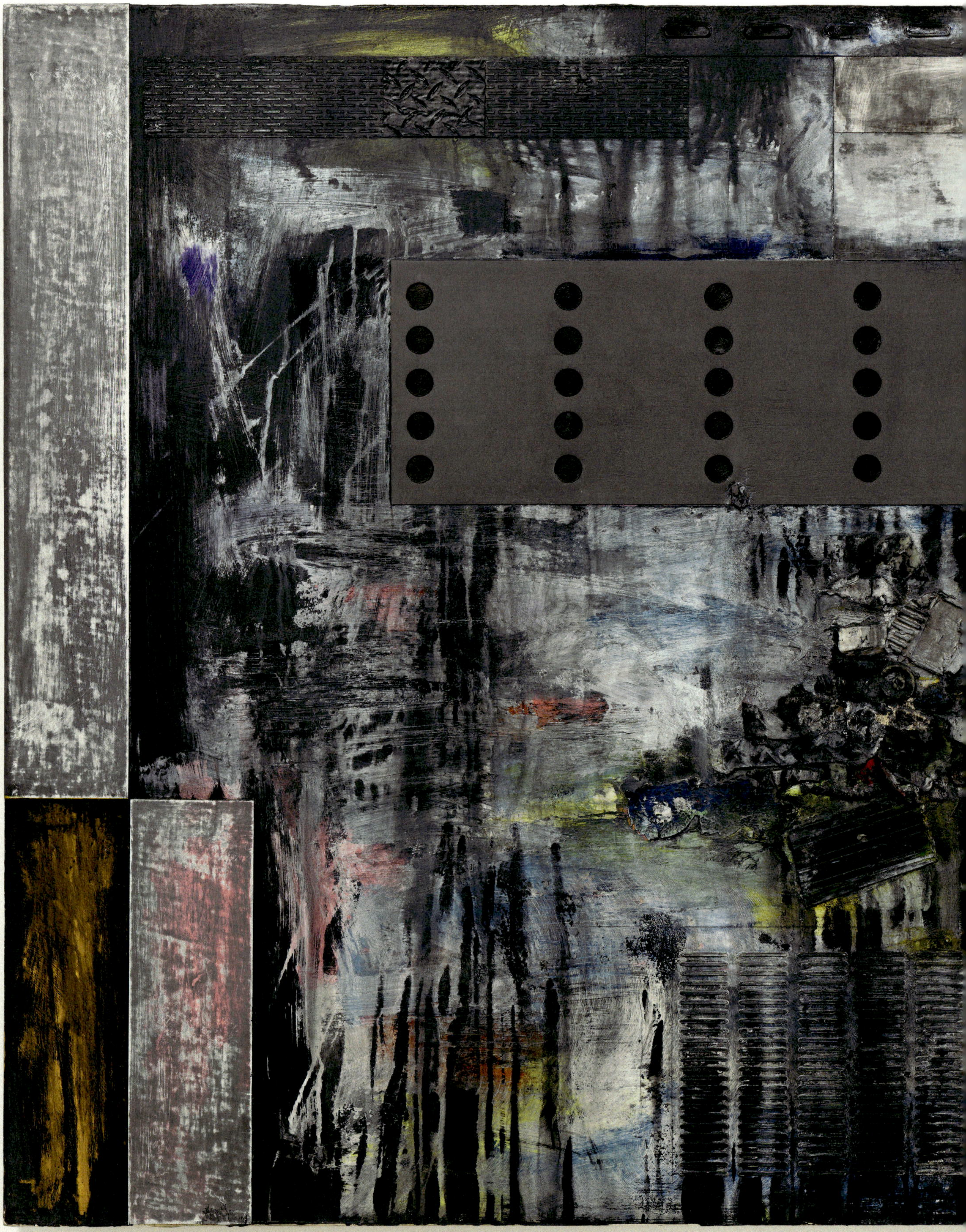

The Gift: Dedicated to the Memory of Packy, 1988

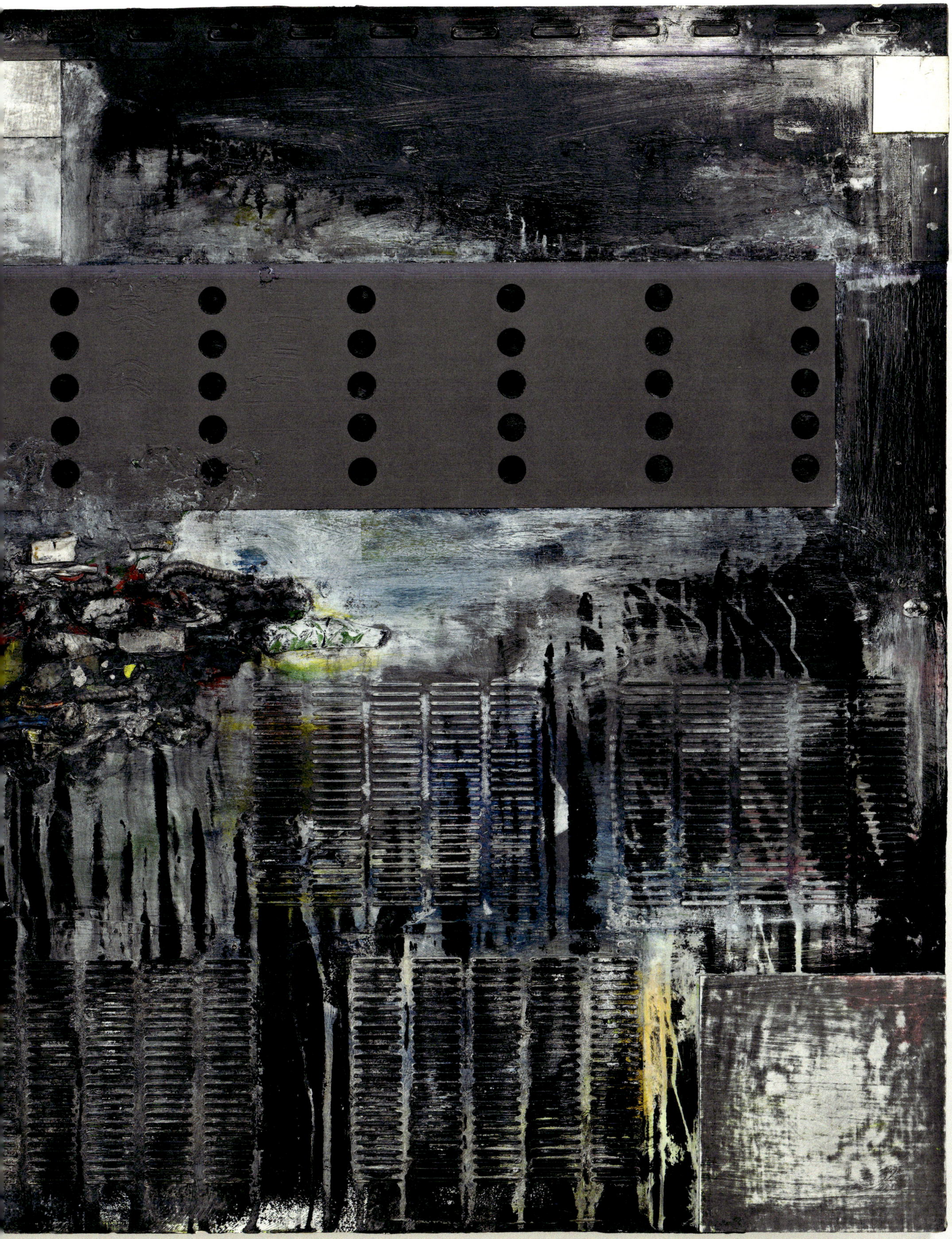

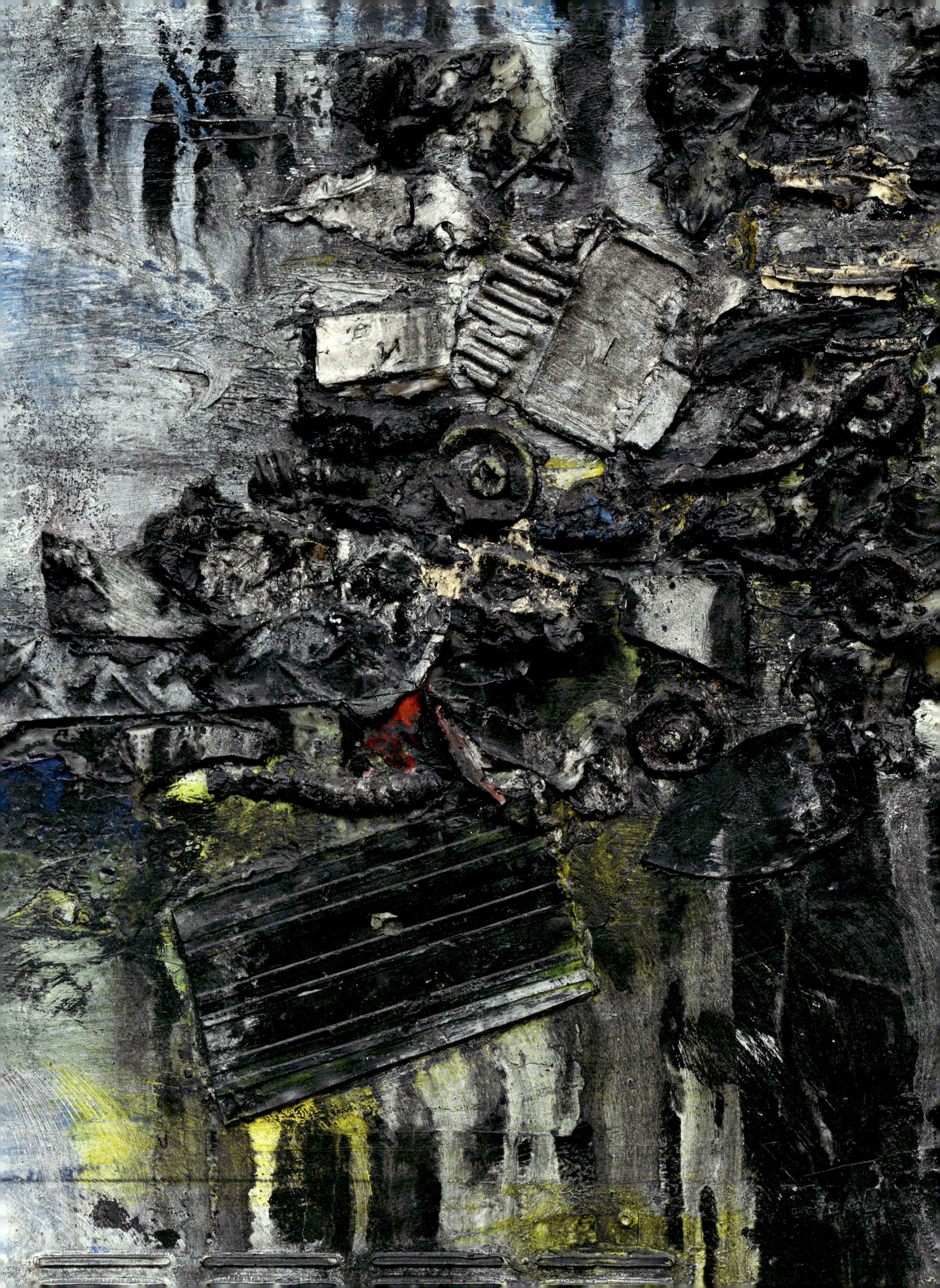

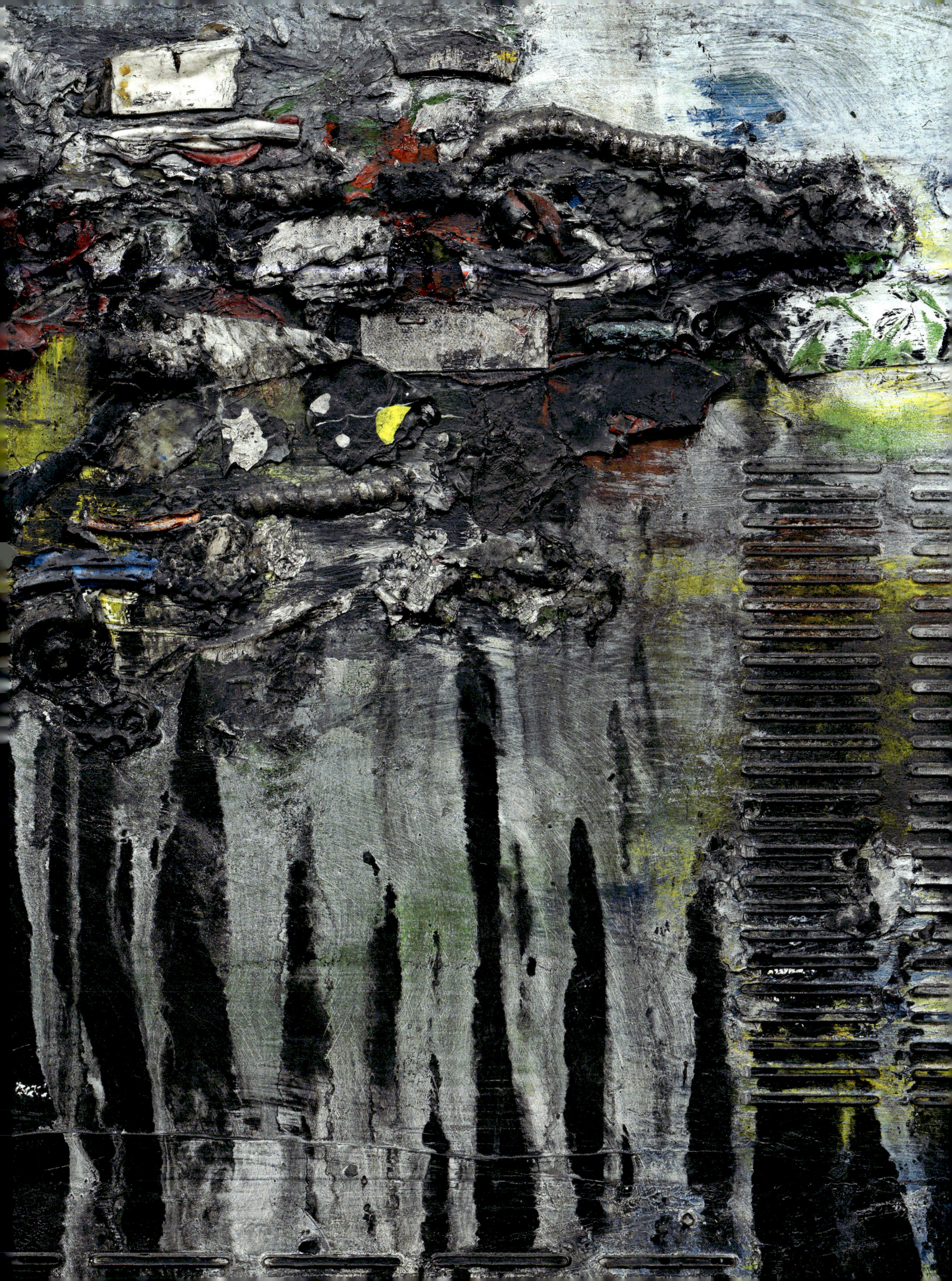

Black Monolith I: A Tribute to James Baldwin, 1988

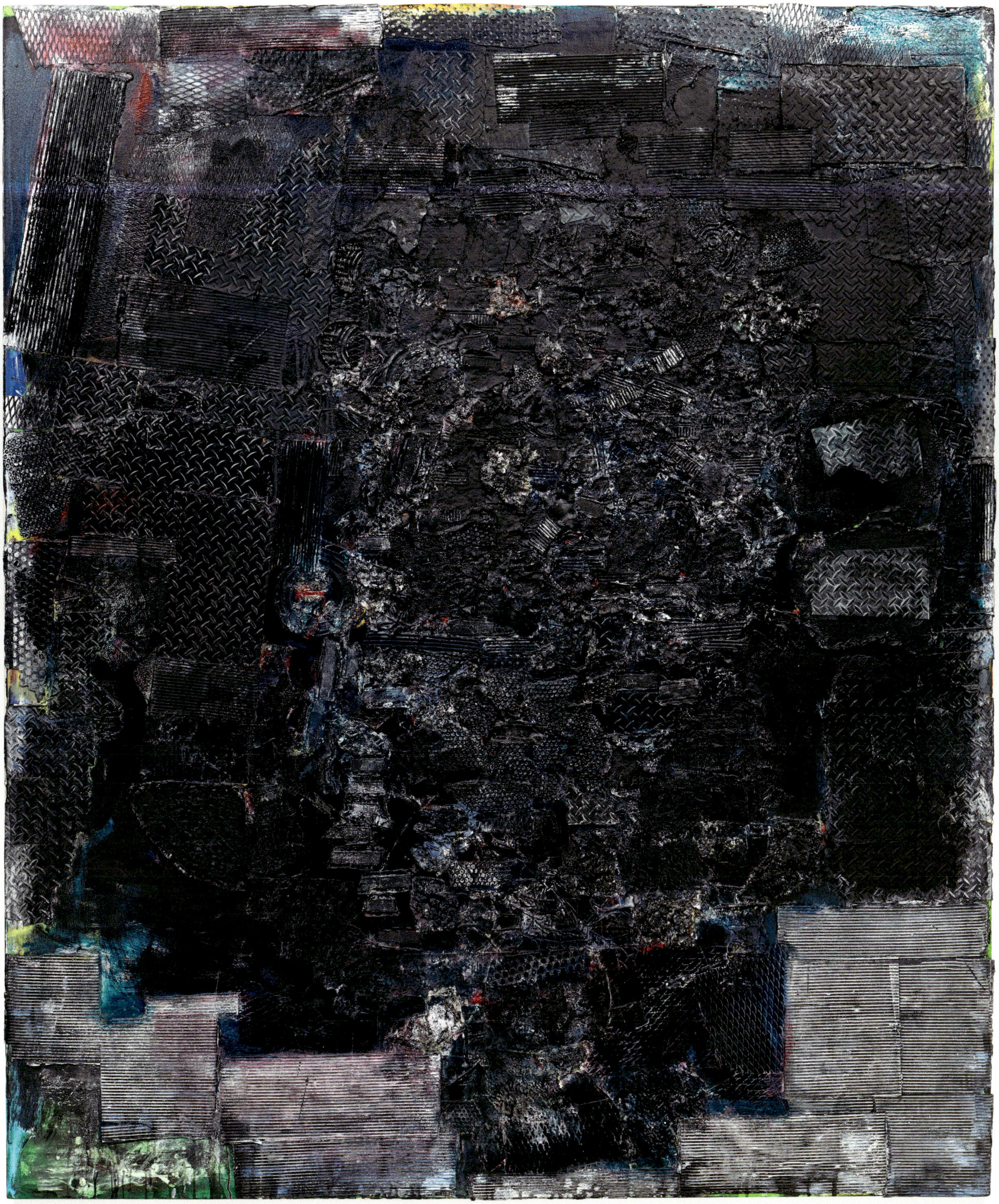

The Burial, 1989

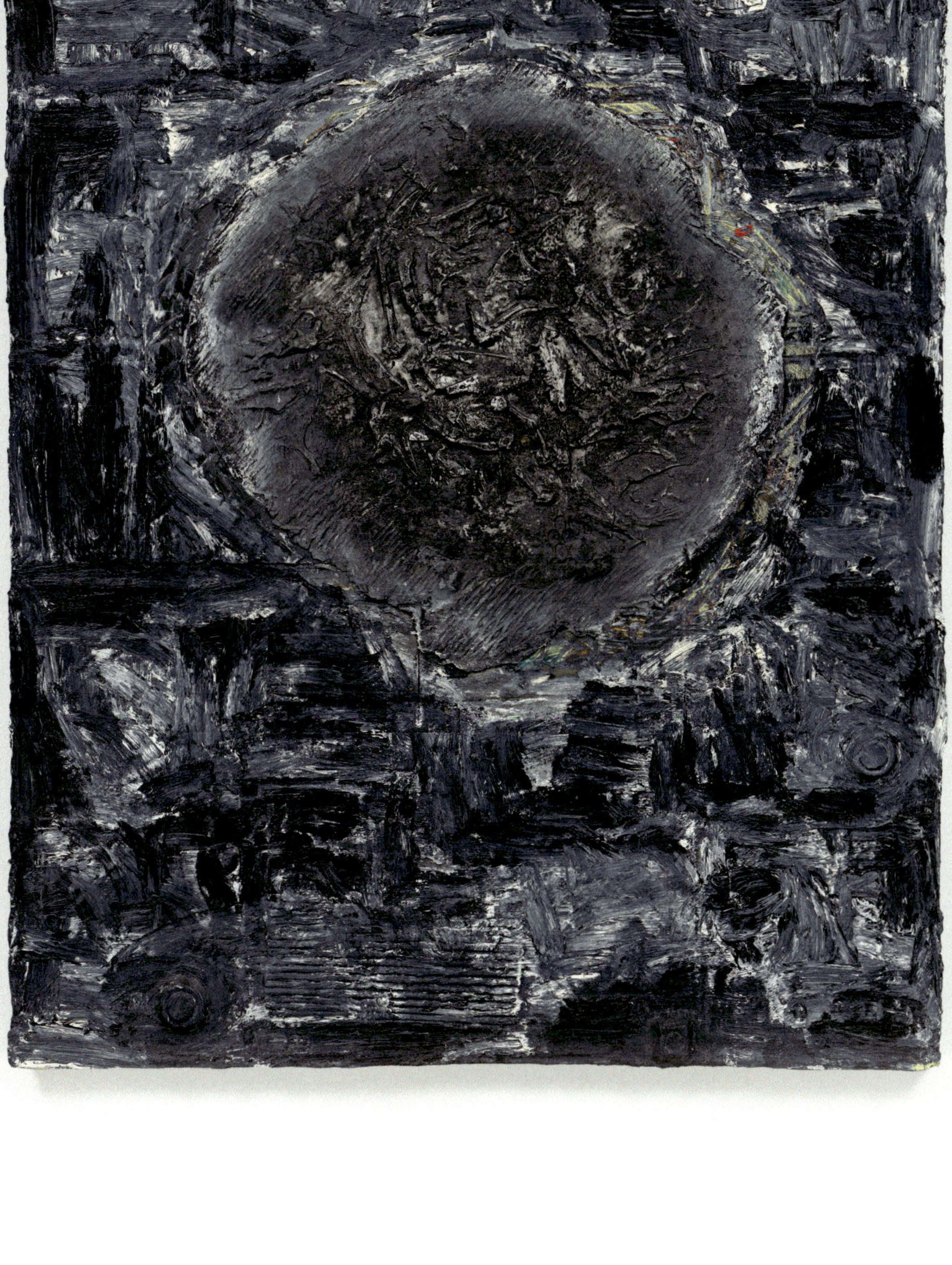

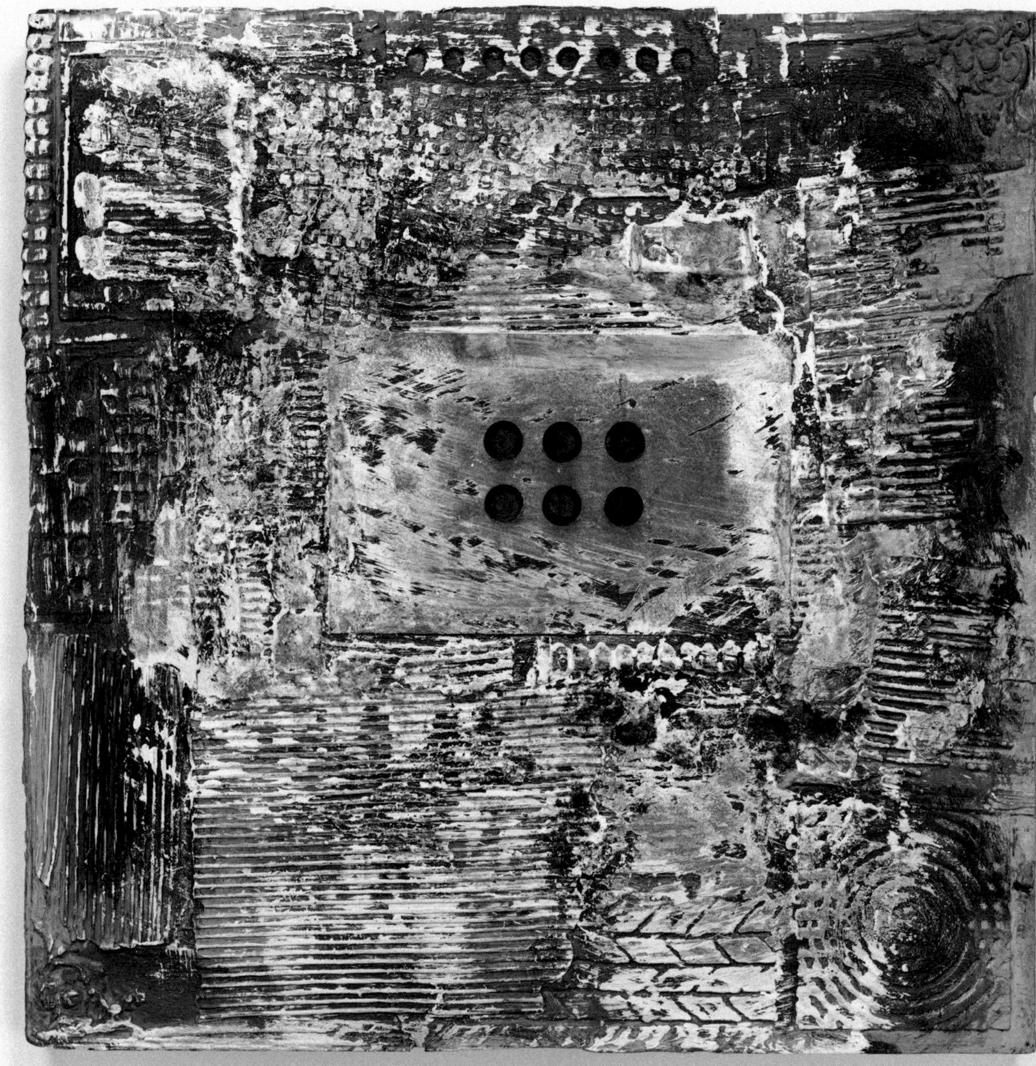

The Offering, 1989

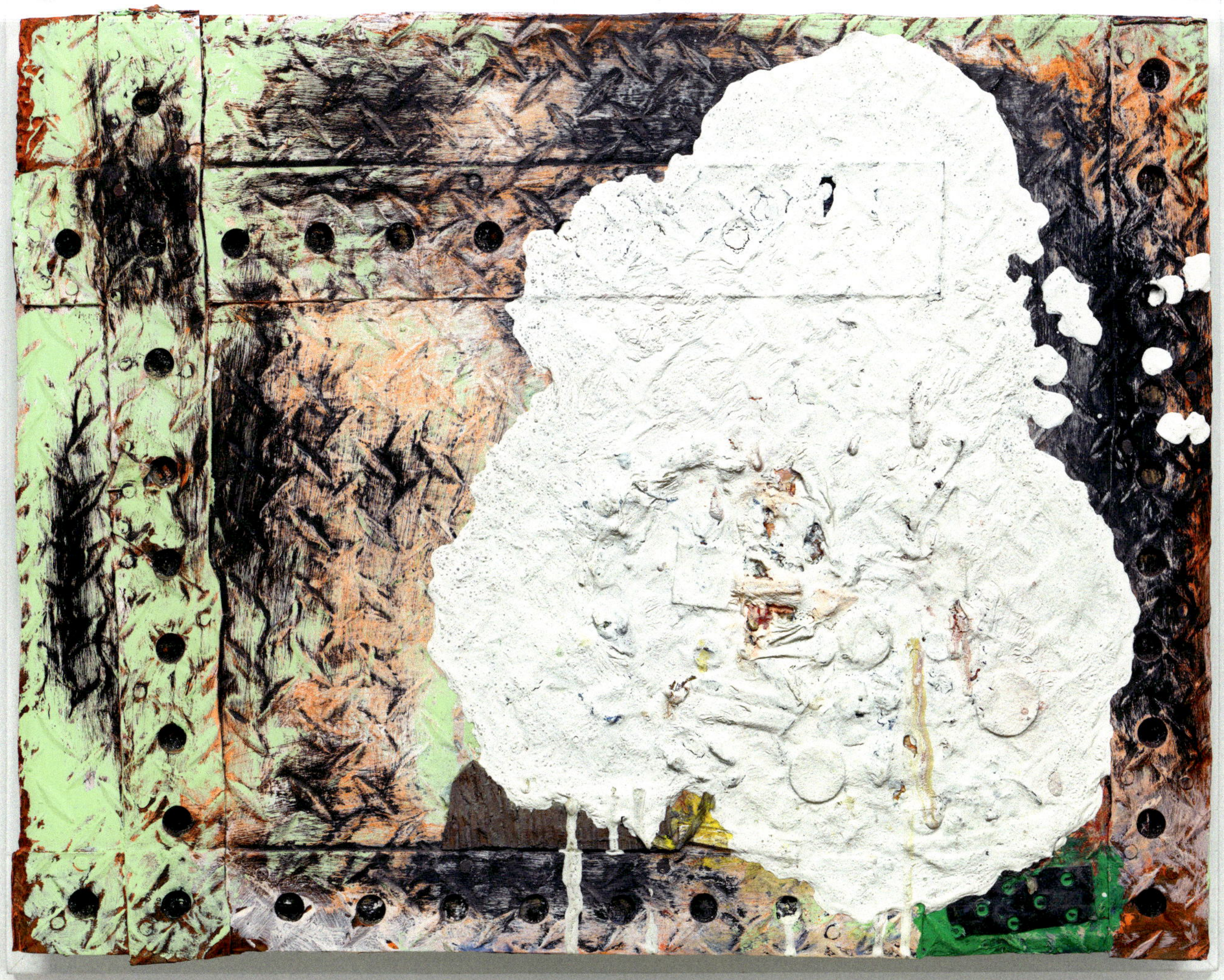

Ecdysis I, 1989

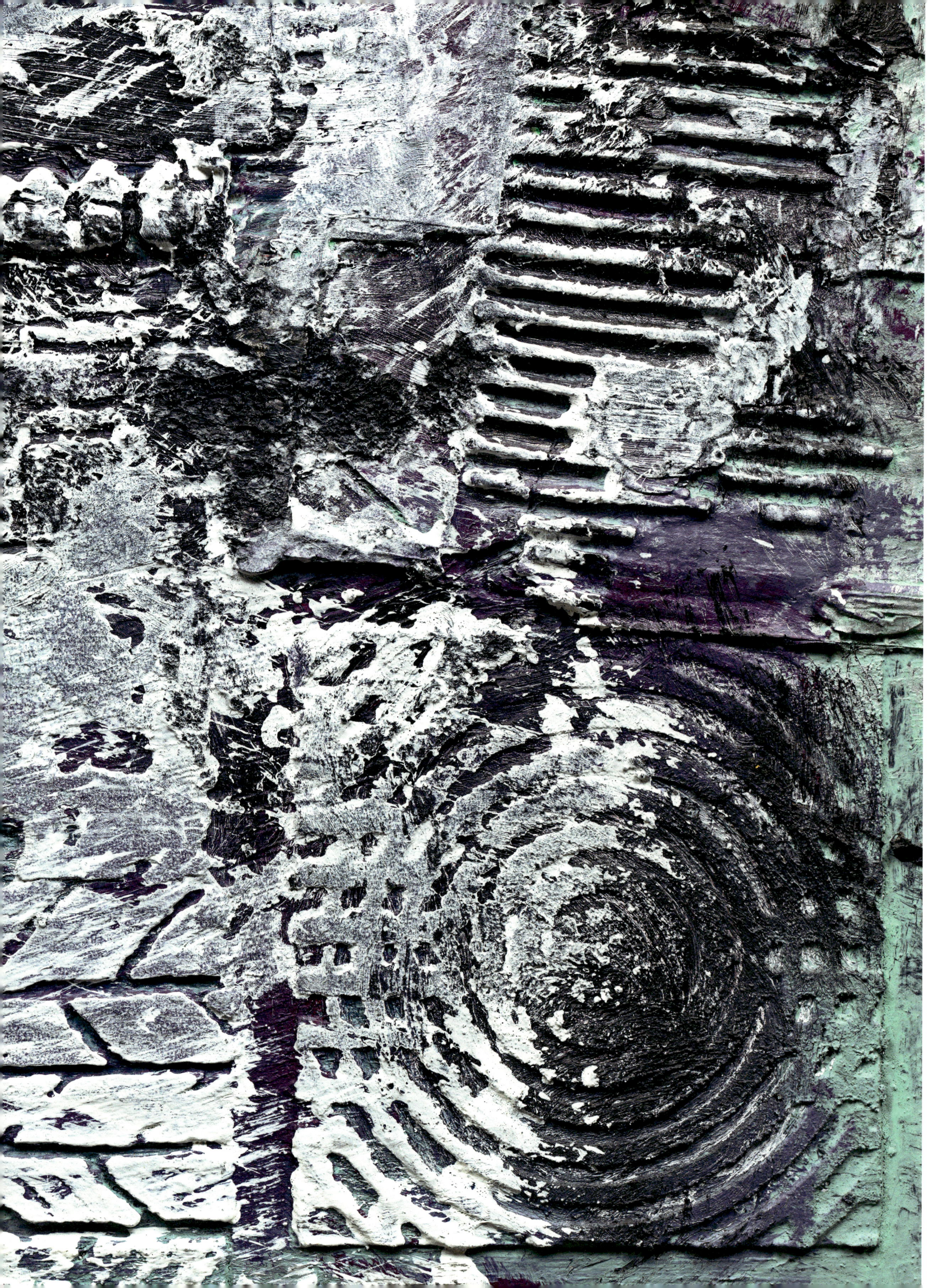

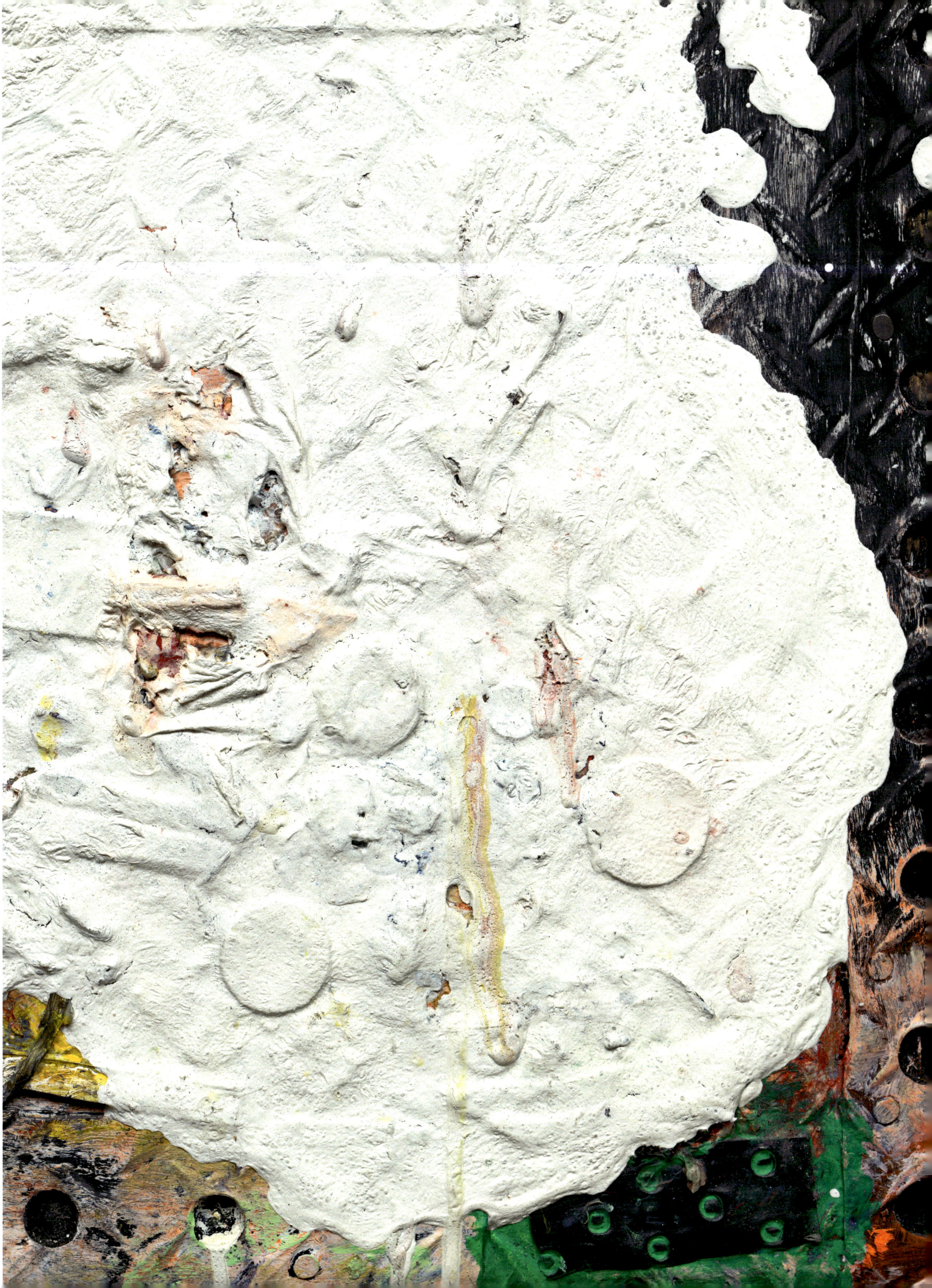

T. History has exhausted all other pos

Therefore, the subject matter must be d

what confuses me or baffles me is thr

eed something other than the formal quan

oes this make me a "Formalist" I wa

econd generation Formalist? Can I, or is there

an paint as a medium, a vechicle f

) sidestep Idea?

If it's possible to concieve of I

playing? This is where I am confused.

within the contradiction of picturialness as

The Abstract Expressionists were wrong

is only the medium and I am the direc

hat remains an unknown, a mystery, but I a

mitation placed upon the spirit. The amaz

ne. It can be animate or inanimate. T

ut I recognize its power and I w

n which mankind finds itself in today

t I feel that our survival as a people

exits. Only the spirit remains free.

spirit. The paint as material is only

estion "Can I go directly to the spirit?"

es of paint? If paint in its "formalness"

about this. Is it possible that I am

way to bypass the formalist approach alt

me directly in touch with spirit? Ho

STUDIO NOTES

the I as medium, what part is the f

ed to objectness lies a presence ... .

inking that the paint was the subject

do not know what form the spirit t

ow that it might take any form: There

t bizarre freedom of the spirit is wh

I find bizzare, and I don't know the med

how can I use it to help the prec

dont want to seem corny or prepost

end upon it.

12 Feb '79

"Free at last! Free at Last! Thank God Almighty
I'm free at LAST" so said Martin Luther King. Jack
Whitten is now saying the same thing. <u>I AM FREE
OF ART HISTORY</u>. At last I am off the floor,
it has been ten years of hard labor on the
floor. I can now execute my works to the wall. There
is no limitation upon scale. The whole significance
of my <u>physical grids</u> is <u>visual atomic structure</u> very
much the same as band-day dots in photography. This
explains the connection to photography. Since 1965 I
have insisted that the image was photographic but I
did not have a clear understanding of what I meant.
The emphasis must not be placed upon the "image"
but as usual upon the plasticity of meaning in terms of
painting as a medium (painting is the medium not me!)
Chuck Close is illustrating what I am saying. He deals
with art as the illustration of an idea. I am vastly
opposed to this thinking. <u>The idea</u>, the <u>concept</u>, the
<u>execution</u> ~~serves only one purpose~~ cannot be separated
from painting as an activity.... the making of a two-
dimensional plane stretched on a support in order to
give rigidity to the plane. We cannot discuss which come
first the painting of the idea. They are totally dependent
upon each other. The attempt to separate leads to illustration
+ design and prevents the activity of art making. Art simply

SL027-1

February 12, 1979

runs out of the window. I think that all great artist have always understood this. When we are reduced to illustration we lose the meaning of Art.

P.S. strange that this should happen on Abe Lincolns Birthday... My freedom is his birthday Present!

SW27_2

24 oct 79

I am still working with a small scale. 16" x 16" – 19 x 19". I don't have
much time to paint and the paintings are changing rapidly, so the
small scale is a must. I was reading Barney Newman's Book and he speaks
of his major problem being what to paint. I agree with this.
What to paint is my major problem at present. So far, I am sticking
to geometrical figures – squares, rectangles – but I don't feel this
to be my real image. Things on the street still excite me, like shapes
of paper sometimes torn edges or irregular shapes. trash from
packing crates – paper – rags. I still insist ~~that~~ upon abstract
painting, the image must be of abstraction as a manner of choice. It
is possible for me to use a figurative image but what's the point!
If figuration does not appeal to me, geometrics does not
appeal to me nor surrealistic dream image (subconscious imagery)?
What's available? Simply stated my interest is to paint the
square, to paint the rectangle without putting anything into
it. That is impossible. How does one paint the square without
resorting to minimalist reductionism? There is something I want to
say about the square of rectangle without showing anything. I keep
going back to African sculpture: the element of an object possessing
a presence. I don't want to put anything into the square, but
the square in order for it to work for me must have a presence!
Obviously I must concentrate upon the total picture plane
without using any dominant figure. The square must dominate.
I could do this by using a mono-chromatic range of all the same values.
This is much to academic and besides some of the early color-field
painters used this idea. I can understand how the Africans managed this
in sculpture: ~~the true dimensionality of sculpture~~ Function played the primary role.
They were built for specific functions and this gave them a built in
plastic structure dependent upon function. In other words form
followed function. I must rediscover the whole purpose of what I am
painting for. What is the function of each piece? Generally
speaking I can say Art for Art's sake or Art's only function being aesthetic.
One thing I do know and that it is necessary. I could mention politics
but I feel the political function of art to be secondary i.e. after
the damn thing is created politics plays its part. The more immediate
function I believe to be personal: First for me and second for the
world. Art must satisfy a very specific personal longing for universality.
over

SU27-8

A desire to feel completely satisfied. A part of the total structure of things. Abstraction is the only possibility for this type of satisfaction, with figuration we are forever depicting something other than the rock-bottom meaning of universality. For this technological age abstraction is the language.
J. Whitten

LIST OF MATERAALS FOR INTRODUCTORY PAINTING

J.WHITTEN

1 - 18x24 White Stathmore pad (all purpose, or equivalent
brand
4 - brushes for acrylic paints #1 #3,#5,#8

Acrylic Paints in Studio size tubes

1 - Cadium yellow light
1 - " " medium
1 - " red light
1 - " " medium
1 - " ornage
1 - Cerulean blue
1 - Ultramarine blue
1 - Alizerin Crimson
1 - Large white
1 - Burnt sienna
1 - Thalo green
1 - Raw umber
1 - Diox purple
1 - Rose,accra violet, or bocour red
1 - Black
1 - Permanent green light
2 - Straight edge razor blades
1 - Small Elmer's glue
1 - 24" metal ruler
1 - Disposable palette
1 - 3/4" masking tape

Canvas and stretchers to be purchased later in course.

5427-9

14 March 80

I always have the feeling that I am getting closer to something to what, I don't know, as if the next painting I will arrive. Arrive at what? What is it that drives me & keep my expectations up? Surely I must learn not to ask this question. Mine is not to reason why.*

The paintings are becoming more joyously. The affirmation of life as Bill Williams put it. Yes, I want to celebrate the fact of my existence to shout hallelujah before all men! Art can be used to glorify life. I want my art to serve this purpose. Death is something unavoidable so why must we celebrate it or mourn it or expect it. When death comes, I am ready. Glory be to Life!

The show at P.S. 1 has really taught me a lesson. My work cannot be shown under those circumstances. I know that already but I continue to exhibit with Black shows for political reasons. I can never expect anything from such shows. My work does not fit into the present category of Black art. I make no associations with African tribal art or derivative motifs. Of course I know the connection between my art & Africa but it's useless to explain. For the sake of simplicity I simply say "It has the spirit" but beyond the emotional impact of the visual experience can anyone see the connection in terms of perception? I maintain that African wood carving is a three dimensional graph the cubical structuring of such is the molecular structure of perception in other words, the unity which exist in African wood carving is the same unity which defines the same energy which defines the universe as a whole. The two-dimensional graph serves the same purpose, which is the same structure found in photographic ben-day dots. In my recognizing this simple fact and using it in my work explains my connection to African tribal art.

Fortunately for me at this time in history the significance of this discovery will play an important role in defining the identity

SL034-1

of the new man. The onslaught of technology presents all of us with a new sensibility, a new esthetic, hopefully a new society with new values. I believe that the present emphasis placed upon art works of obvious "primitive" character is a direct result of this "new man vibration". In other words, we read the vibration to mean a new society with new myths new symbols, a starting from the beginning...... the present day artist will create the new symbols needed for a new society. My African ancestry places me in a better position to take advantage of this new man mentality. I more than any man represent the new race. I am the product of all men. I do not share the guilt of Christianity nor the burden of Capitalism. My spirit is one of freedom forever seeking the heights above mans folly and mans inhumanity to man. Mans greed make war necessary. How true, back in 1964 when I painted the canvas Look Mom, Look, see the Funny People! that painting says it all. What am I to do? Must I also drag my spirit into the gutter? I think not. As long as the breath of life generate my physical being I will celebrate mans humanity.

Yes, my art is about self-revelation not to be confused with self-glorification. I use my art to define the self I can only hope that others can do the same. So what drives me? The search, the continuous struggle to define the self. Now, I know that one never discovers the self not in a lifetime nowhere; we discover the self only to lose it. The self is the sands of the river Nile, the Acropolis in Athens, a Congo fetish, a Bill de Kooning Woman #1, a Saturn rocket to the moon, Mt. Everest. The self is all things and many more. More the better, I say, for there is no final chapter.

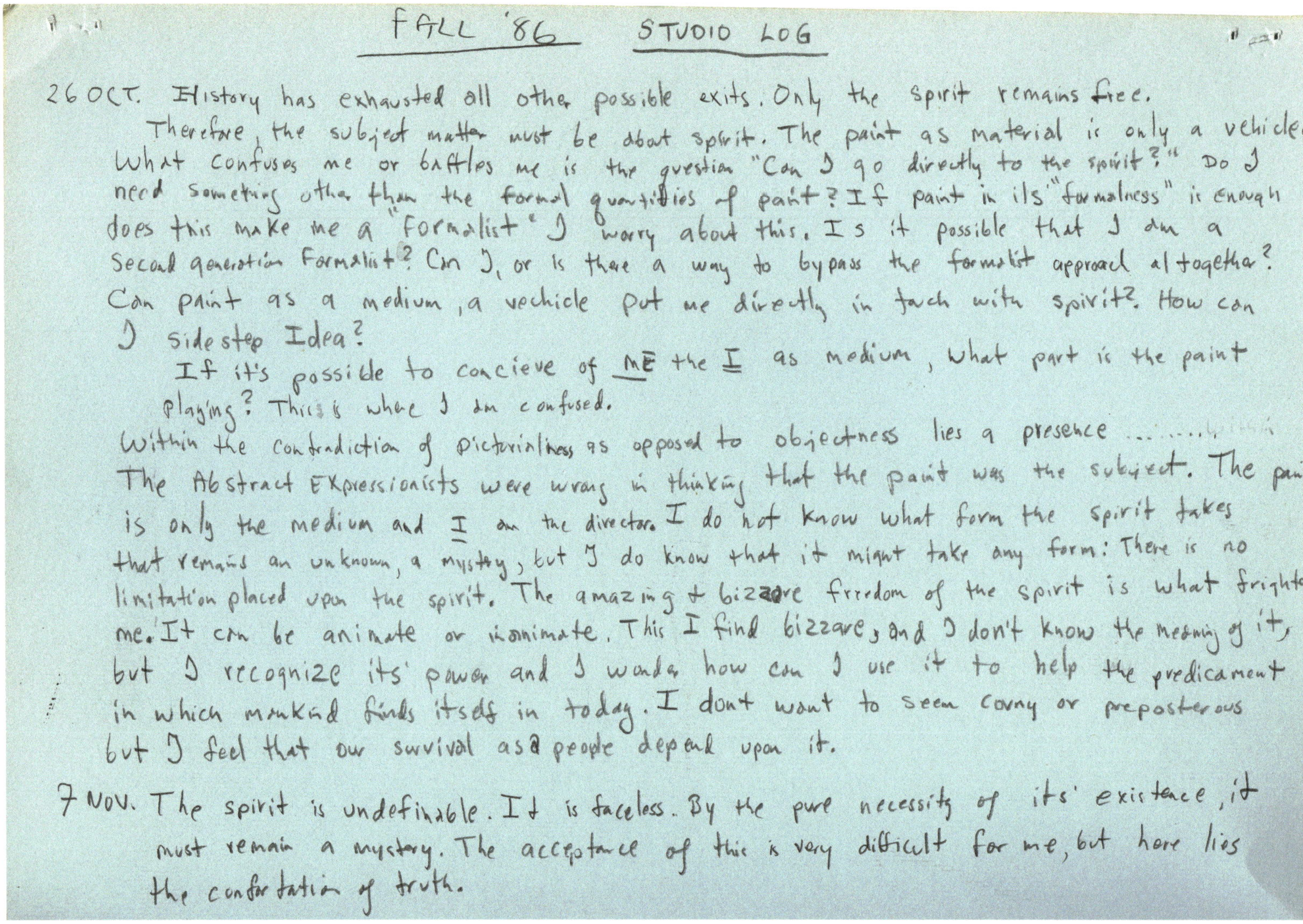
FALL '86 STUDIO LOG

26 OCT. History has exhausted all other possible exits. Only the spirit remains free.
Therefore, the subject matter must be about spirit. The paint as material is only a vehicle.
What confuses me or baffles me is the question "Can I go directly to the spirit?" Do I
need something other than the formal quantities of paint? If paint in its "formalness" is enough
does this make me a "Formalist" I worry about this. Is it possible that I am a
second generation Formalist? Can I, or is there a way to bypass the formalist approach altogether?
Can paint as a medium, a vechicle put me directly in touch with spirit? How can
I sidestep Idea?
If it's possible to concieve of ME the I as medium, what part is the paint
playing? This is where I am confused.
Within the contradiction of picturialness as opposed to objectness lies a presence ....
The Abstract Expressionists were wrong in thinking that the paint was the subject. The paint
is only the medium and I am the director. I do not know what form the spirit takes
that remains an unknown, a mystery, but I do know that it might take any form: There is no
limitation placed upon the spirit. The amazing & bizzare freedom of the spirit is what frightens
me. It can be animate or inanimate. This I find bizzare, and I don't know the meaning of it,
but I recognize its' power and I wonder how can I use it to help the predicament
in which mankind finds itself in today. I dont want to seem corny or preposterous
but I feel that our survival as a people depend upon it.

7 NOV. The spirit is undefinable. It is faceless. By the pure necessity of its' existence, it
must remain a mystery. The acceptance of this is very difficult for me, but here lies
the confortation of truth.

16 Nov. It's a psychic object arrived from the psychic reality.

2 DEC. There must be a visual equivalent to Jazz.
..... an actually object expressing the same pathos.
I want my art to show this.

9. DEC. TIME IS A FRAGMENT OF BEING.

11 DEC. THERE IS NO IDEA. THERE IS ONLY BEING.

14 Dec. I have three possible directions:
(1) I can continue to mix-up the execution
(2). Use of screens to establish a net for trapping images
(3). Direct manipulation of pigment, totally organic

16 Dec. I am beginning to experience full release, something still holds me. I think that politics is an obstacle to growth. My cosmic desire is for full release. I still need more information to be sure. What pain is in store for me? I still worry.

25. It's like trying to see the other side of something, as if a veil of some sort separates me from it.
The molecular structure exist in the form of light not in physicality as previously thought.
The problem at present is that my light source is to fragmented. I need a condenser.

17 Jan 87 The It is an unknown factor. I am dedicated to the preservation of mystery. Only in its' political manifestation is it necessary to remove the mystery. This is the main difference between politics and art. The choice rests with the individual participant.
The clarity of desire operates as an excellent condenser.

18 Jan. YOU NEVER TAKE IT; IT'S ALWAYS GIVEN TO YOU.

21 JAN. I DON'T BELIEVE IN CONCEPTUAL ART; IF YOU CAN CONCEIVE OF IT THEN IT'S NOT ART BUT AN ILLUSTRATION OF AN IDEA.

26 JAN. EXCEPT FOR THE USE OF MATERIALS THERE IS NOTHING RATIONAL ABOUT PAINTING. NOR CAN IT BE CALLED IRRATIONAL; IT EXIST SOMEWHERE IN THE EXTREME MIDDLE.

1 FEB. THERE IS AN EDGE WITHIN THE EDGE.

2 FEB. THE CENTER CAN BE ANYTHING YOU WANT IT TO BE!

3 FEB. THE IDEA IS TO MAKE THE OPPOSITES DANCE, SING A SONG, PRAY AND HAVE A GOOD TIME!

LIST OF WORKS

Ascension I
1979
Acrylic on canvas
64 x 64 in. (162.6 x 162.6 cm)
Courtesy the artist and Hauser & Wirth
page 35

DNA XI
1979
Acrylic on canvas
16 x 16 in. (40.6 x 40.6 cm)
Courtesy the artist and Hauser & Wirth
pages 36, 38

DNA XII
1979
Acrylic on canvas
16 x 16 in. (40.6 x 40.6 cm)
Courtesy the artist and Hauser & Wirth
pages 37, 39

DNA X
1979
Acrylic on canvas
16 x 16 in. (40.6 x 40.6 cm)
Courtesy the artist and Hauser & Wirth
page 40

DNA III
1979
Acrylic on canvas
16 x 16 in. (40.7 x 40.7 cm)
Courtesy the artist and Hauser & Wirth
page 41

Untitled II
1979
Oil on canvas
22 x 22 in. (55.9 x 55.9 cm)
Courtesy the artist and Hauser & Wirth
page 43

Confirmation I: Happy Birthday Mary
1979
Acrylic on canvas
19½ x 19½ in. (49.5 x 49.5 cm)
Collection Mary Whitten
pages 45–47

Black in Time I
1980
Acrylic on canvas
30¼ x 30¼ in. (76.8 x 76.8 cm)
Collection Jack Whitten
page 48

Yellow Cross for Naomi
1980
Acrylic on canvas
42 x 42 in. (106.7 x 106.7 cm)
Collection James Cross
page 49

Annabelle II
1984
Oil and acrylic on canvas on wood
67¼ x 67¼ in. (170.8 x 170.8 cm)
Courtesy the artist and Hauser & Wirth
pages 51–53

To My Valentine
1984
Acrylic and oil on canvas
45 x 45 in. (114.3 x 114.3 cm)
Courtesy the artist and Hauser & Wirth
page 55

Soweto Disk II AKA Big O for Obama
1985
Acrylic and shoe polish on canvas
89½ x 89½ in. (227.3 x 227.3 cm)
Courtesy the artist and Hauser & Wirth
pages 57–59

The Kid from Red Bank: The Count
1985
Acrylic and oil on canvas
89½ x 89½ in. (227.3 x 227.3 cm)
Courtesy the artist and Hauser & Wirth
page 61

Norman Lewis Triptych I
1985
Oil and acrylic on canvas
28 x 81½ in. (71.1 x 207 cm)
Courtesy the artist and Hauser & Wirth
pages 62–65

Site I
1986
Acrylic on canvas
14½ x 9½ in. (36.8 x 24.1 cm)
Courtesy the artist and Hauser & Wirth
page 67

Site IV
1986
Acrylic on canvas
84 x 72 in. (213.4 x 182.9 cm)
Courtesy the artist and Hauser & Wirth
pages 69–71

Ode to Andy: For Andy Warhol
1986
Acrylic on canvas
96 x 82 x 2 in. (243.8 x 208.3 x 5.1 cm)
Courtesy the artist and Hauser & Wirth
pages 73–75

Willi Meets the Keeper (For Willi Smith)
1987
Acrylic on canvas
96 x 82 x 2 in. (243.8 x 208.3 x 5.1 cm)
Courtesy the artist and Hauser & Wirth
page 77

The Alliance
1988
Acrylic on canvas
48 x 82 in. (121.9 x 208.3 cm)
Courtesy the artist and Hauser & Wirth
pages 78–79

The Gift: Dedicated to the Memory of Packy
1988
Acrylic with cast acrylic collage on canvas
48 x 82 in. (121.9 x 208.3 cm)
Courtesy the artist and Hauser & Wirth
pages 80–83

Black Monolith I: A Tribute to James Baldwin
1988
Acrylic on canvas
96 x 82 in. (243.8 x 208.3 cm)
Courtesy the artist and Hauser & Wirth
page 85

The Burial
1989
Acrylic and oil on canvas
30¼ x 27⅞ in. (76.8 x 70.8 cm)
Courtesy the artist and Hauser & Wirth
page 87

The Offering
1989
Acrylic on canvas on board
26⅛ x 26⅛ in. (66.4 x 66.4 cm)
Courtesy the artist and Hauser & Wirth
pages 88, 90

Ecdysis I
1989
Artist collage on plywood
16¼ x 21¼ in. (41.4 x 54 cm)
Courtesy the artist and Hauser & Wirth
pages 89, 91

Published on the occasion of the exhibition *More Dimensions Than You Know: Jack Whitten, Paintings 1979–1989*, presented at Hauser & Wirth London, September 27–November 18, 2017

Exhibition organized by Richard Shiff

Editor: Richard Shiff
Managing editor: Diana Murphy
Project assistance: Sara Sohye Chun, Michael Plunkett, Jake Brodsky, and Cory Reynolds
Design and typography: Rita Jules and Miko McGinty
Pre-press: prints professional, Berlin
Production coordination: Nadine Engler and Christine Stäcker
Printing and binding: DZA Druckerei zu Altenburg GmbH

Cover: *Site IV*, 1986, detail
Page 2: Jack Whitten in his studio at 36 Lispenard St., New York, 1983, photographed by Peter Bellamy
Page 4: *The Kid from Red Bank: The Count*, 1985, detail
Page 32: *Ascension I*, 1979, detail

Illustration credits:
© 2017 The Barnett Newman Foundation, New York / Artists Rights Society (ARS), New York: 23; © 2017 Peter Bellamy: 2; Renderings by Jake Brodsky: 18 left; Photograph by Julian Calero: 22, 49; © 2017 Rena Effendi, National Geographic Creative: 28; Photographs by Genevieve Hanson: 4, 6, 11, 20, 27, 32, 35–41, 43, 45–48, 51–53, 55, 57–59, 61–65, 67, 69–71, 73–75, 77–83, 85, 87–91; Photograph © 2017 Museum of Fine Arts, Boston: 10; Courtesy Jack Whitten: 8, 12, 13, 17, 18 right, 19, 26; © 2017 The Willem de Kooning Foundation, New York / Artists Rights Society (ARS), New York: 9

Cataloguing-in-Publication Data is available from the Library of Congress.

Available in North America through
ARTBOOK | D.A.P.
75 Broad Street, suite 630
New York, NY 10004
Tel 212 627 1999 | Fax 212 627 9484

ISBN 978-3-906915-06-7

Printed and bound in Germany